Life Decisions

Wanda Maria Phillips

A-RIA Publishing

Life Decisions

ISBN: 978-0-9787920-0-8

Printed in the United States

Disclaimer and Limitation of Liability:

This book is designed to provide information and resources about the subject matter covered. The author is not rending professional advice.

The fact that an organization or website is mentioned does not mean the author endorses the information or services provided. The resources mentioned in this book should be evaluated by the reader. Readers should also be aware that organizations and websites mentioned may have been changed or ceased operations since the publication of this book.

Every effort has been made to contact cited quotes for permission of use.

To order additional copies of this resource or more information, please visit: www.expressionsoflife.org

Table of Contents

Introduction 7

Mirror Reflection 8
   Looking glass into your soul 10
   God's Reflection 14
   The Inner You 17

   Career 20
   Finding your job 21

   Career Choice 24
   Trusting God for you Future 26
   Hey Look Up 28

   Portrait of Success 31

Pay day who wants to be a millionaire... For God 37
   Tithe or not to tithe that is the question? 38
   Give back to God 41
   Budgeting your life 43

Life's little crisis 46
   I am about to explode! 48
   Why wait?...No one else is 52
   Stop the pain.... Please! 57
   What are you high on? 61
   I just want to belong 64
   Violence is raging 68

Relationships 70
   Friends today, gone tomorrow 71
   Friendships made by God 75

   The hook-up! 78
   Single and mangling with God 81

   Are You Marriage Material? 85
   Forgiven... but not forgotten 88

Family Dynamics 91
  You just don't understand do you? 93
  Why do you hurt me then leave me? 97
  You're Not Really My Parent 100

Sharing the word 102
  Love one another 103
  So, you want to join? 106
  Praise God I belong, now what? 109

Conclusion 112

Resources 113

Life's Decision Journal

This book is dedicated to my heavenly Father from whom all blessings have truly flowed. To my awesome husband Eugene "Geno" many thanks for your support, encouragement, guidance most of all for your unlimited love as I took on this great challenge. I love you with all my heart! To the most precious gifts from God, our children Adrian and Maria. I love you both dearly! A special thank you to my parent's Charles and Dorothy Young for all you've done and given me in my life. It is with much gratitude that I say thanks and especially to my mother. Mom, you taught me to be strong, caring and loving. These qualities instilled in me are part of what continues to drive my actions. You have always been supportive even when you may not always see, or understood my visions. To my late grandmother Myria Lee; who showed me in her daily walk with God what a true strong woman of God looked like and how to become one. I give you as well, much love and respect for your love, teachings and example. I have no doubt that you are looking down each day and hour when I praise God's name in all that I do, think, and speak. I would also like to thank all of my family each one of you has a special place in my heart. Although my sister Cynthia would prefer me not to use the term Editor; I thank her for assuming and taking on my asking her to review my work and make suggestions. Thank you for your time, listening and giving valuable and useful advice. You are not only my sister, but my friend who has stuck with me through it all. I love you Sis! I want to thank my sisters in Christ Sherlette, Toni, Danita and Mama Doris for their encouragement, friendship, and the laughter you provided just when I needed it the most. To all the wonderful people at Five Star Salon, St. Peters, Missouri, thanks for the ministry of laughter and words of wisdom from God. To my sounding boards, Mia and Paula; thanks for always being there and available whenever I needed you or your support. To all those mentors that helped me in my ministry may God continue to rain blesses down upon you. To Pastor Dr. Harvey Fields Jr. and my Union Baptist Church family of Chesterfield, Missouri; I owe you much love, gratitude and thanks as you allowed me to grow, participate in sharing God's word, and spreading my wings in the Lord. Thanks so much for opening the doors of ministry and teaching, giving me another start toward my journey. It is with much appreciation that I give thanks to all the women of Union Baptist for your support, love, and respect as I try to run this race.

To Pastor, Rev. James E. Lacy of First Baptist of Creve Coeur, Missouri, I thank you for believing in me enough to ask and allow me to teach such a dynamic group of young adults. It is because of these young adults that I finally acquired the thought and courage to write this book.

To all the teens and young adults I have ministered to on this journey; I thank you for the opportunity and want you all to know how much of an impact you have made on my life. I extend my love and prayers continually for all of you. Remember to keep your head up, look always to God who is your source of strength, direction and guidance from today, tomorrow, and always!!

Introduction:

As a Teen, or Young Adult various things cross your mind as you enter in High School or upon finishing your High School journey and approaching with great thought the next step in your life. The first step is coming to a place where you are confident and secure in who you are before you can move into other areas of your life. Whether you are still in High School, coming to a decision about your future, electing to enter college, get a job, learn a trade, or enter the Military; you must examine a career path to walk and your next steps. There is the issue of dealing with different relationships that will be encountered in your life. You will also be presented with decisions about dating; staying single or to get married in the future. As you tread into this new and exciting phase of your life you also have to deal with different twist and turns that arise as you take these next steps. But, remember all these steps are to assist you in moving through your teen years into adulthood. Whatever path you chose, there will be all kinds of questions and decisions and yes, disappointments which may cause some anxiety. The feelings you have are normal, remember we are talking about moving into adulthood and becoming a young adult. The question now is how do you manage all of these new changes and still live a Christian Life? Together we will explore and see how God can and will enhance your character. You will learn how God can help you to reach out to others and strengthen your relationships. You will also discover how to be a Christian and still have a fun filled and enjoyable life. Prayerfully, you will realize that being a Christian does not mean that you cannot still have fun; it just means you'll have to find activities that represent your Christian Character.

Well, with the Divine Spirit of God and a little humor prayerfully I can at least make an attempt to assist in some of your questions and maybe reflect on some not mentioned yet. Becoming an adult is a challenging journey, but extremely rewarding as you achieve all God has planned for your life. Let's get started on our journey and help you put on the gear which is the armor of Christ as you begin, or continue your walk with God.

Mirror Reflection:

> **For it is impossible to be**
> **in the presence of Jesus**
> **and not be changed.**
> **Joanna Weaver**

As you enter into your teens, young adult and adult life, it is always good to reflect on your past, but not dwell on it rather move forward toward your future. We must all learn from past mistakes in order not to repeat them. First, you must examine the qualities that make you who you are. God has made you in His own image, but it is up to you to make your life in the image of Him. We must also use the microscope of God's love to look into our inner soul and review those actions, and feelings that cause us not to see God's reflection in us. Then you must realize that God doesn't make mistakes, and has created you in the most wonderful beauty imaginable. Once we build ourselves up in His image we will find the joy in all that we approach, and we will achieve great things in His name. **The Lord is my strength and my shield; My heart trusted in Him, and I am helped; Therefore my heart greatly rejoices, And with my song I will praise Him. Psalm 28:7 NKJV**

In the lessons to follow, we will take time out to really look in the mirror and find out how God could have made such a wonderful mold of Himself in you. We will learn how to become more like Him and to appreciate what He has made with us. You have to learn to stop looking at yourself as the images that the world has conjured up, but the image that God has for each one of us. When you take the time to look in the mirror and see through the eyes of God, we will only see the magnificent image that He views. By looking through God's eyes, you will realize that with every flaw you think is seen, it's only the touch that God has put on us to make each of us as unique and a brilliant creation.

We must get past the point of being concerned with what others think, or feel about us. A master craftsman has made us, God, our Father. God envisions us all as individuals with different skin tones, body types, features, thoughts, dreams, goals, and destinations. You must learn to appreciate what you have been blessed to become. You must also watch being envious of how others look; for the same people you might be envy may not like who they are either. Much of time the ones that seem to have it all going for them turn out to be the ones who feel just like you do. They too perhaps like you don't feel worthy, attractive, or even loved for who they are as an individual. Often those that everyone may feel has it all, might deal with as much pressure as those that feel they don't have it all. When you put anyone on such a high pestle, there are those that are watching, judging and waiting for you to fall. For example: If you are considered to be built really nice, the minute you gain some weight or start to lose that muscle, some may start to criticize you. This causes pressure on them. This could cause them to go to the extreme to lose weight by binging and purging, eating very little or even nothing at all. In some, it could cause them to take drugs to help them build up. In either case, what they are trying accommodate is what others think they should be. This is no different than those who feel like they are different; both groups consider themselves inadequate As Christians we must realize that there is nothing wrong with how God made you, what is incorrect is that we allow others to determine are worth, value and beauty. God made is to be just who we are and that's what is most important, because He only makes exquisiteness. So why don't we check out God's brilliance and the flaws we think we see, let's see how they are seen through God's eyes.

Your beauty should not come from outward adornment, such as braided hair and the wearing of gold jewelry and fine clothes. Instead, it should be that of your inner self, the unfading beauty of a gentle and quiet spirit, which is of great worth in God's sight.

1 Peter 3:3-4 NIV

Lesson 1
Looking glass into your soul

As a young woman I spent my whole childhood being self-conscious of a skin disorder called vitiligo. This disorder can turn your skin a different color. In my case, it created white spots on my face and fingers. As a child and a young teen, kids made fun of me and they made me feel horrible. It was as if I had a disease that they could catch. As a young adult and adult I felt unattractive. I believed that I would never date, have a boyfriend, or even get married. I had forgotten that God had made me and He doesn't make mistakes. Even though I questioned His artwork of me, I thought maybe He forgot to use the right material. He couldn't have possibly wanted me to live or feel like this the remainder of my life. I had forgotten that God had a plan for my life, but until I started to feel good about myself, I could never fully experience what God had in store for me in my walk of life.

No matter what the world may see or like, it's about what God designed. It is not about your size, hair, skin, or overall appearance; it's about the inner beauty shinning through, making you the wonderful person and presence here on earth. God made us all unique and different for a reason. Because of this, we must embrace the beauty in us and know that we are special and loved by God. It's the inner you that can change the outer you in a positive, or negative way. You can be the most beautiful person in the view of others on the outside and have a negative attitude and personality that makes you very unattractive. Yet, you can have a wonderful attitude and presence and be the most attractive person in a room. Once we realize that the very being of our soul truly reflects what is seen, more time will be spent developing the inside, rather than concentrating on the outside appearance. We must search the inside of our soul to bring forth the beauty that God intended for the world to see.

Therefore, it doesn't have to be a skin disorder that could cause one to look deep inside themselves. It could be mental or physical abuse you may have suffered. It could be someone saying something negative about you, or it could be a learning, development, or emotional disorder that may be causing these emotions. Whatever the reason for your feelings of self-consciousness, feeling unattractive, unintelligent, lonely, misunderstood, unlovable, guilty, or any other negative thoughts or feelings you have felt, or you are feeling in your life; there is someone who can help you change those emotions and thoughts. God has seen your heart and knows what you have been through and He sees the beauty in you. God sees the type of beauty that magnifies through you and is seen or observed by others.

The type of beauty that destroys all of those flaws you think are seen are those negative statements you have heard, or even said to yourself. We must realize there is nothing out there that can make you perfect to the world. But you are perfect, because you're exactly the creation God intended. God is the only perfect one. His love for us, and that love made us in His image of perfection.

For example, when a jeweler examines a gem which may have imperfections, those flaws don't keep it from being a stunning jewel. The eyes of God and Him alone know our true flaws, but some of those same flaws also make you unique and different. No one wants to have the same gem as everyone else they want something unique and different. That is why you are a precious gem to God because of what He created in and through you, which is more special than what the world thinks or says. You are a unique find which embodies all of who and what God planned for you to become, so shine like a diamond in the sky.

God wants you to feel His love and He wants you to know that your soul beautifies who you are.

Your eyes saw my substance, being yet unformed. And in Your book, they all were written, The days fashioned for me, When as yet there were none of them. Psalms 139:16 NKJV God already knew what you would become before you were ever formed. It is your responsibility to communicate with God to see what He distinguishes special in you. You must believe that God only wants the very best for you. God never pushes Himself or His will on you. He gives you free will, and opportunities to fulfill the destiny He has planned for your life. Know that you have been given the capabilities to achieve all that God has planned for your destiny. It is all within you: the courage, strength, beauty, love, self-esteem etc. You simple have to believe and know who you belong to and that is God your Father, who has made you after His own image. When you realize that you matter especially to God, then the world better look out because God's child is coming through and there is nothing beyond your reach.

Deal with yourself as an individual worthy of respect and make everyone else deal with you the same.
Nikki Giovanni

God,

Our prayer is that the things that are thought of as imperfections; will become seen with our eyes as what is making us into the wonderful gem that you created us to become.

Amen

QUESTIONS:

1. When you look in the mirror what do you see?

2. How do you think your past experiences can help form your future?

3. Name five things that describe you?

4. What things would you like to change about yourself?

5. Who can make you feel worse; you, other people, or both?

6. Who do you think should make you feel good about yourself?

Lesson 2
God's Reflection

But God has revealed them to us through His Spirit. For the Spirit searches all things, yes, the deep things of God. For what man knows the things of a man except the spirit of the man which is in him? 1 Corinthians 2:10-11 NKJV. God looks into the same mirror as you look into except He only sees a perfect child of His. Yes, He knows all of your mistakes and all the accomplishments you have made and the ones you will accomplish. You must let go of the past failures and forgive yourself. God has already forgiven you of all of our past mistakes. God's word tells us that: **If we confess our sins, He is faithful and just to forgive us our sins and to cleanse us from all unrighteousness. 1 John 1:9 NKJV** When you look into the mirror you should see God's reflection looking back at you not your past, but your future in Him. We must remember we all have a history with good times and hard struggles. Nevertheless, both experiences build our character and make us who we are and who we will become. God never promised that we would not have hard times, but the word lets us know that He will be with us always even to end on time. Some of you may have experienced abuse or know of someone one who has. You must remember that it was not your fault, but abuser's fault. God will give you what you need in order to come from the ashes of despair and rebuild you even stronger than before. The God that made us is the reflection that we should envision for ourselves which represents: purity, goodness, and love. You should always remember you're a true representation of God no matter what you have been through or what others may say about you in past or future.

Despite what you have been through, God still wants to use you to be a blessing to someone else. You may wonder why I went through these struggles; you may even ask where was God? You frequently hear Pastor's say, "In order to have a testimony you must have a test or you will just have a moaning. We all have our own mountains to climb, but with God we can soar to the top. If you never gone through anything in your life wouldn't know who brought you through, and that could have only been God. You are never alone He is always there and sometimes He even carriers you when you can't take another step. After God delivers you take those experiences to help someone else get through similar situations.

Let others see through your testimony that no matter what circumstances arise in their life they can make it by holding on to God's hand, just like you did. Now look in the mirror and see that God is looking right back at you. You can make it because Christ is in your heart. **The Lord Does not look at the things man looks at. Man looks at the outward appearance, but the Lord looks at the heart. 1 Samuel 16:7 NIV**

QUESTIONS:

1. What issues have caused you not to see God's reflection?

2. What types of characteristics of God would you like to have reflected?

3. What struggles helped to mold your character?

4. What helped you to get through your struggles?

5. Did you ever feel that God had left you?

Lesson 3
The inner you

We must continue to ask God for wisdom and insight and for the strength to persevere. He will cause us to rise up and fly like eagles, walking and not fainting. Norma Smalley

Let's go and examine the place where no one can see, sometimes not even you. The place where you may have experienced different types of emotions of: hurts, disappointments, rejections, sadness, loneliness even in a crowded room. The place that we share joys and sorrows alone because we feel as if no one else seems to care or has time for us. The place in your heart and mind that made you feel inferior to others you're around. There may also be an area of your life where fear of the future and past insecurities reside. We have all been in these places within ourselves at one time even if we don't want to admit it. If you haven't felt this way keep on living. We sometimes feel as if the world is crashing in and you don't know where to turn. Life is exiting, but with it comes challenges, what we have been through, or what we are going through which can put additional strain in situations that occur in our lives.

Nonetheless, we have the strength through Christ to be over comers. We can face our past fears, insecurities, emotions and become stronger from them. First, we must take time to examine ourselves and all those things we have pushed far back trying to make them go away. The things that creep up in new relationships, and other new challenges we try to approach. Until you find out what makes you fearful, insecure and emotional, you can't let them go. If you have pushed the feelings too far back, ask God to reveal and help to remove them from the inner you, so you can truly become what God had planned. We must also ask God to help us conquer challenges that may come into our lives that could bring back all those negative feelings, or thoughts. **The Lord will give you strength unto his people; The Lord will bless his people with peace. Psalms 29:11 NIV**

You can't let others determine your worth. The world has made us feel that if we don't look, live, drive, or have certain things we aren't living up to their standards and expectations. Even as Christians we sometimes judge others based on the way we think someone deserves to be blessed. God has given us all special gifts, talents, and it up to us to find them through His guidance and develop them to their full potential.

You are more than your looks, where you live, and the family you come from. God has given us all the ability to achieve great things through Him. We all have to learn not to judge others, or even ourselves. We have all made mistakes, but they don't define the outcome of our lives. As a child of the most High, the Lord our God we must see beyond the past to move into the future that God has planned for our lives. You must take the first step by believing that your past is only the path to your future. Each stumbling block is just a little road bump that you will go over and reach your destination that God has planned for your life.

God,
I pray that you will touch and heal the inner me. Help and give me strength to move towards all the Blessings you have in store for me. Allow me to become strong in you and grant me the knowledge of your word to help me grow. Please help me to learn from my mistakes, but not be defeated by them. Thank you for the road that you have paved for me if I follow you on this walk.
Amen.

QUESTIONS:

1. What have you pushed back?

2. How can you change the negative feelings you may have?

3. What makes these feelings resurface in your life?

4. Who can we share these feelings with? Name at least two if possible?

5. Do you feel others understand your feelings? If not, why?

CAREER:

It's now time to get paid. You are preparing for that future by courses you have selected, interest you're developing, or jobs you have taken after school or during the summer. Maybe you finished High School, and or you have taken on adult responsibilities and making adult choices. Now what are you going to do that will make all your dreams come true? Well, some of you will be heading off to college while others will be attending vocational school, going into the military and some will be heading straight into the job market, or some may even decide to become entrepreneurs. Whichever avenue you have chosen, I am sure you want to know how to get paid and how much will you get paid. Yet a few will just want to go into a career that will bring fulfillment and joy. We must realize that no matter what is decided; when you put your mind to it and with the help of God anything can be accomplished.

Even before you jump on the avenue of life, you need to check and see who will be your boss and what might be the job description. The most important step before you choose your path is to make sure you have God as your guide and the Bible as your map. All avenues are open to you if you follow your guide God and His road map for life, the Bible. If you want to make a name for yourself, first make a name with God. After you do that, the world is yours for the taking, because God is directing you in the correct direction. When, you realize that in order to truly get somewhere new in your life, we all need direction and guidance. Once you maintain a relationship with God, He will direct your path and you will be successful. **Commit to the Lord whatever you do, and your plans will succeed. Proverbs 16:3 NIV** You can now get the bling bling and more! When you put your trust in God, it's like having your own navigational system of life. All you have to do is submit your destination and God will give the best directions to get there. So, let's start our journey; don't forget to enter your destination with God and wait for the correct direction and enjoy where you arrive.

Lesson 1

Finding your job

Take time to reflect on your interests. For an example, do you like helping people or do you enjoy working with children? You should find the interest that gives you much joy. Commit it to the Lord and let Him direct your path in achieving that goal. God has a place for you that will take your interests, skills, and educational background and direct you toward a job situation that will magnify Him and bless you. But, you must put God in the front of your decision making and not an afterthought. Just think of God as your job counselor, tell Him what you are looking for and what you have to offer. Then pray and let God guide you in selecting job opportunities. That doesn't mean you don't have to look for work because remember what the word states; **And I say unto you, Ask, and it shall be given you; seek, and ye shall find; knock, and it shall be opened unto you. Luke 11:9 KJV.** As Christians we sometimes think we can just ask and it will be automatically given to us. This is not how God works in our lives; He gives us what we need at the right time.

The word says, as the body without the spirit is dead, so faith without deeds is dead James 2:26 NIV. We show through our actions how much faith we have in God. Once you put your trust in God your behavior should show the faith that you have in Him. We must put effort toward what we have asked God to grant us. If you have asked God to bless you with a job and you haven't done anything to obtain the job then why should God bless?

You need to prepare yourself through training, education, or a willingness to learn along with prayer. Then submit your application, resume, and follow up with what you submitted. Next, be prepared for your interview. In doing so you must be professional, courteous, and most of all represent your father well. You have to put everything into obtaining the job you have asked God to bless you obtaining. When you show God your faithfulness to Him and what you know He can provide for you, He is touched by your real faith. We must remember God is not our genie; He doesn't just go around granting our every wish.

God sees all and knows all that is happening in our lives or will happen. Sometimes what we want isn't good for us, or may later turn out wrong for us and that's why we don't receive it because of that very reason. God gives us freedom of choice, but He will present opportunities for you to choose. That is why it is so important to have God as your job counselor, and any job counselor will tell you to give your best and you will be rewarded.

God has given each of us the opportunity to become all that we can. We have to always remember that in order to have success; he or she must have an attitude and desire to succeed. You have to want great things in your life, and then believe that, and you must not give up.

Whatever you do, work at it with your heart, as working for the Lord, not for men since you know that you will receive an inheritance from the Lord as a reward. It is the Lord Christ you are serving.
Colossians: 3:23-24 NIV

QUESTIONS:

1. What interest do you have?

2. How can you develop your interest to make it your career?

3. What are you seeking in a job?

4. Is there anyone helping you with your job or career search?

5. If yes to the above question have you talked with the person yet?

6. Would you allow God to help in your job or career search?

Lesson 2

Career Choice

From the word of God, it lets us know that: **A man's heart deviseth his way, but the Lord directeth his steps. Proverbs 16:9 KJV** This informs us that God has already ordered your steps. God has given each one of us a talent, a special gift and when you use your talent for the glory of our Lord you will be richly blessed. God can use you in a job to make a difference in His Kingdom here on earth as well as in Heaven. If you have a relationship with God it will last a lifetime. Then He will guide you toward your career. Even though our careers may change the relationship with God will last and He will continue to be our guide. **Make level paths for your feet, and take only ways that are firm. Proverbs 4:26 NIV** We walk different paths in our lives moving in different directions, but all should be working towards God's will for our lives. When we are in God's will we succeed and glorify Him. So no matter what choice you finally make; as long as God has guided you there you're already on the firm path. Along this journey you will realize that God uses everything in our lives to magnify Him; our careers are just one of the expressions of His purpose in our lives.

An unknown author said, **"Don't let yourself become so "hung up" with a particular job that you neglect your relationship with God."** Each place of service is an opportunity for God to fulfill His purpose through your blessings. When God puts you in a position, it is for you to reach out to those who don't know Him. No, it doesn't mean you have to preach to them, but the light God has instilled you should outshine the brightest star. When the world sees you, they should see something special and different about you, and how you handle your job and your attitude lets others know you are a true child of God. So, let your path magnify God, and He will richly bless you.

QUESTIONS:

1. What goals have you set for yourself?

2. What do you feel are your assets and how can they be used to achieve your goals?

3. Has God begun to show you ways He might use you with a career choice to make a difference for His Kingdom? Jot down what they are below.

4. Do you feel that you can allow God to direct your plan even if you don't know what the outcome may be?

Lesson 3
Trusting God for your Future

For I know the thoughts, I think toward you, peace and not of evil, to give you a future and a hope. Jeremiah 29:11 NKJV God is perfectly capable of guiding your life so that you are effective in the work place to glorify Him. God knows what will happen even before you start toward your career or endeavor. You just have to continue to pray for guidance and correct attitude. We all know how unpredictable the job market can be with downsizing and layoffs, but we know that God has already blessed your steps. **The Young lions lack and suffer hunger; But those who seek the Lord shall not lack any good thing. Psalms 34:10 NKJV** God only asks that we have faith and trust in Him with all that we do, say and think. If we believe in Him, great things will be achieved and in achieving them, we will magnify Him. When God blesses us, we are a testimony of what He is able to accomplish. Once you have removed yourself as the driver and allowed God to take control, get ready for the ride of your life. Now that Christ is the driver and you are the passenger, let's sit back and see where you will go and what all you'll achieve, if you just trust in Him. The paths that have been chosen for us can lead us in wonderful directions if we put our trust in God. Remember, **Trust in the Lord with all your heart and lean not on your own understanding; in all your ways acknowledge him, and he will make your paths straight. Proverbs 3:5 NIV** So, jump on the road of life with Christ and enjoy the ride.

God,
As we move forward in seeking your guidance in our career choices, please show us your will. Lord show us please how to minister to those we come in contact with as we go into our careers.

Amen

QUESTIONS:

1. When you look at your future, do you believe God has a plan for you?

2. Do you believe that God will provide you with job opportunities?

3. Do you believe God can use you in the work place? Why or why not?

4. Whose hands have you put your future in?

5. What do you sense God wants to do with your life?

Lesson 4

Hey! Look Up!

Lift up our eyes your heavenly Father waits to bless you in inconceivable ways to make your life what you never dreamed it could be.
Anne Ortlund

We must remember that scripture states: **But my God wants to supply all of your needs according His riches in glory by Christ Jesus. Philippians 4:19 KJV** These words include providing provisions through your job opportunities. However; you must be willing to look to God to reveal His will in your life. God will reveal His will through the Holy Spirit. The Holy Spirit can speak to you through the Bible, and through prayer by giving you scriptures to minister to you. For example, you are deciding if teaching is the career for you. The Holy Spirit can speak to you through the Bible, by giving you scriptures to minister to your heart about teaching. When you are praying about teaching or a teaching position, God can also give you peace when you seek His guidance on choosing this job or career. You may have an opportunity to participate in church, or event and afterwards someone may comment on how well you relate to others and how they enjoyed listening to you speak. This may be God's way of revealing to you that you are on the right path at pursuing teaching as your career.

The Holy Spirit works together with the Word and Prayer to bring you to what God has in store for your future. God's revelation in your life can give your vision and goals so much clarity. Once you look up you can feel His presence and you can then find peace with your decision. God's word shares this: **The secret things belong to the Lord our God, but the things revealed belong to us and to our children forever, that we may follow all the words of this law. Deuteronomy 29:29 NIV** God is waiting to enlighten you and all that is required is for you to just look up and He will shine down your blessings.

How many times have we just been complacent in our situations and unable to move forward? We spend so much time looking down and feeling down, that we don't even look up. We need to understand the source of our blessings starts by looking up to God. I believe that when praises go up, blessings do <u>come</u> down. Just like the rain on a warm day, like white snow on a winter's day, God has proven that when we look to Him for the answers; He will shower us with guidance and love in order to grow and become like a wonderful flower that grew after the rain.

When you are in doubt of what to do, where to go, or how to behave; just look up and seek the guidance from God. He is the one who holds our past, present, and future; and He is waiting for you to just look up and receive what is destined for you. Don't forget what God has for you is specifically for you. Hey you, just look up!

QUESTIONS:

1. Have you let the Holy Spirit guide you?

2. Have you seen God work through the Holy Spirit in your career choices?

3. What confirmations has God shown you regarding your career goals?

4. Have you looked up yet? What has shined down?

Lesson 5
A Portrait of Success

For no man can be blessed without the acceptance of his own head
Yoruba Proverb

It's funny how society rates success. If you are a college graduate or higher and earning top dollar, own a nice car and house, then according to society standards you are considered successful. Don't get me wrong, there is nothing wrong with having all these material possessions. Your success should not solely depend on acquiring these things. It's how you earn them and the type of life you live once you have obtained them. You should live your life by standing for something and not falling for just anything.

There was a time long ago when Minorities couldn't receive these types of things, despite less opportunities they still had a wonderful life. There have been strong individuals that used their skills and intelligence to achieve great rewards. Where would we be if there were no electricians, plumbers, chefs, police officers, firefighters etc.? These people may not have gone to college, but learned hands on from one generation to the next. Maybe they learned their skills from a trade school or Military training. We must realize that a person's worth is determined by how much they put into achieving their dreams. Their ultimate goal was to learn all that they could in order to be the best in whatever he, or she does.

Your attitude about who you are and what you have is a very little thing that makes a very big difference. -Theodore Roosevelt

How many times have you allowed other's thoughts and beliefs keep you from achieving your goals? How many times have you stopped believing in yourself because things got too tough? I can relate to having all of those feelings. I allowed how others felt about my appearance and intelligence to determine how I felt about myself.

As pre-teen, I let the teasing of the other kids drop my self-esteem to zero. I believed them when they said, "no one would want to be around me because of my skin disorder." I let them make me feel so self-conscious that I wouldn't let anyone into my life, fearing that they would treat me the same as those kids. It is true that kids can be cruel. I carried those feelings into everything I attempted. Then I become a young adult and allowed those feelings cause me to make wrong choices; I wanted to prove that I was wanted and loved. When I finally looked back, I realized that trying to prove them wrong only made things worse and it's made me realize how I disappointed God and myself.

It is not always appearances that can make you have low self-esteem. You may be dealing with some other issues in your life that you feel are impossible to overcome. What makes you stand out from what others think is how you turn it around. You must believe in yourself even when no one else does. Believing in yourself is about knowing that God has something special in store for you. Once you believe, all things can be achieved with help from God and your faith. Life will always present those who will cross your path with negativity and judgments, but remember that their thoughts and attitudes can't keep you from obtaining all that is there for you to obtain.

You may need to be persistent, work a little harder, seek assistance and guidance to achieve your dreams but it will be conquered. The day will come and you won't have to say a word; but your light will shine and the world can see that you are more than a conqueror; you're an achiever.

As you move forward in life, you may need to become your own cheering squad. I was blessed to have two wonderful people in my life; my mother and grandmother. The foundation began with my grandmother "SUG." This is what everyone called my grandmother. She was a strong, unique, gifted, and spiritually centered person. Over time, I saw myself taking her attributes and implementing them in to my life. I became founder and member of "SUGS" Squad; A strong, unique, gifted, and spiritually centered young lady. It took me a long time to arrive at that point in my own life, but I learned a lot from her. She didn't let her lack of education, or where she came from keep her from becoming all that God meant her to become. My Grandmother showed me that you might be a single parent and raise a fine child that loves God. She showed me that you could have a business mind and become an entrepreneur and that you could run a household and be a servant of God. She showed me that you could be a missionary here at home. God took an old country girl and turned her into a woman that started a generation of strong determined individuals. Her legacy lives on through those who came after her. Just as she did, each one of you can and will provide the next generation with their abilities and give guidance. The question is what legacy will you leave? Will it be one of achievers, or quitters? Which category do you rank?

My husband always says, "A failure is only one who quits." I am writing this book because I refuse to be a quitter again, in my life. Even though there are those that may doubt or feel that I may not be educated enough to write, teach, Minister or whatever is being thought. It's not about them but what my God feels and thinks of me His child.

It is my responsibility to share the message that He given me to share with each individual that is reading this book. I stand on God's word: **Jesus looked at them and said, "With man this is impossible, but with God all things are possible." Matthew 19:26 NIV** I had to learn as you must, that it's not about what your educational background may be or have been, it's about what you want to accomplish to glorify God and represent yourself. You can take what you have been given and expand on it to achieve such great things in your life.

I once read an African-American Folklore that said, "God makes three requests of his children: Do the best you can, where you are, with what you have, now." God has a perfect plan for our lives if we follow Him and His will.

For some of you may be equipped with college, trade, or military experience while others may have world experience, or hands on education. It is about taking what you have to help provide for you and perhaps maybe a family. It's about what you can give to others through your knowledge. It's not about having a College degree or not, but what you do with what God has given you. You must remember it's in your court to continue to educate yourself and others with your knowledge. We should never look down on someone or make him or her feel inadequate if they haven't obtained a certain type of education or skill. I once remember an older person saying, "There are a lot of educated fools." Education is to enhance you, but common sense sustains you.

You may ask why I feel so strongly on this subject. Well, I am one of those individuals I was a year and a half away from my degree; I stopped school to work and then later raise a family. I always heard that if you don't receive a degree in a field they you will be unable to reach your professional goals. My husband who is a College graduate and a business owner said to me," that it's not always about having a degree, but the desire and the willingness to want to learn even if just through hands on experience." Now don't get me wrong, I will encourage you as well as my children to attend College and pursue a degree if that is where your path leads. However, I also realize that every child is not bound for College. They may be blessed to start a business, go into as professional sport, or even choose to take up a trade, etc. The most important thing is that whatever accomplishments you are trying to reach, take God with you and your will reach the top. Can you feel me?

I am taking my own advice and making sure that I continue to learn and grow in the field that I am interested in pursuing. You can never have enough knowledge about the path you are interested in following. The most important part is that I am including God on this journey to reach my dreams and goal, and I'm giving it my best.

So, let's get moving and reach, attain, and complete those dreams. Don't let anyone turn you around. It is never too late to reach for the stars. Remember the words of God, **All hard work brings a profit, but mere talk leads only to poverty. Proverbs 14:23 NIV**

Take a day to heal from the lies you've told yourself and the ones that have been told to you.
Maya Angeloou

Questions:

1. What do you think makes someone successful?

2. Do you believe that success is only achieved through financial gains?

3. Has anyone made you feel unsuccessful?

4. Why do you think society has a limited view of success?

5. Do you know someone who has achieved success without a formal education?

Pay Day!
Who Wants to Be a Millionaire For God?

We all have dreams of finding that great job or coming up with the right concept that will make us millions. We forget that money can't make you as rich as knowing God. When you learn to live for God; He can make all of your dreams come true. However, you must first learn God's ways and allow them to become part of your everyday living. You must learn this in order to receive good gifts. You must first be willing to give because it all comes from God. **"Give and it will be given to you: good measure pressed down, shaken together, and running over, shall men give into your bosom. For with the same measure that you use, it will be measured back to you." Luke 6:38 NKJV**

Sometimes we need to stop and look at what we have and thank God for these blessings. Then, we need to make sure we are giving back with our tithes, time, talents, gifts, and love. God has such wonderful blessings in store for you and material things are just a small part of an even bigger picture of His eternal love for us. So, before you move into these next lessons, I pray that you open your <u>mind</u> and heart to the Lord and watch how God not only blesses you, but how He will also bless your finances. He will bless you beyond anything you could ever imagine and in ways you never thought about. God will use people to help you when you can't even help yourself to maintain a wonderful life. Why not become a millionaire for Christ? That is the biggest payoff you could ever receive in your Christian life.

God lets us know that having riches is great, but having eternal riches are the ultimate reward. **Do not store up for yourselves treasures on earth, where moth and rust destroy, and where thieves break in and steal. But store for yourselves treasures in heaven, where moth and rust do not destroy, and where thieves do not break in and steal. For where your treasure is there your heart will be also. Matthew 6:19-21 NIV**

Lesson 1

To Tithe or not to Tithe that is the question?

When I wrote the first version of this book it was cut and dry you pay 10% of your gross salary, or amount given to you. However, as life has molded me and I have read and heard different discussions on tithing; I have grown to understand more about the real topic on tithing. I still believe that you should give back what God has given you, but my knowledge has increased on what is considered the amount to give. We really need to understand more of what God had in mind when He talked about tithing. We must also understand how we have gotten away from what God really had in mind about tithing. We have made people feel that if they don't tithe 10% they won't receive blessings. What God wants us to know is that tithing establishes a relationship with Him. **You may say to yourself, " My power and the strength of my hands have produced this wealth for me," But remember the Lord your God, for it is he who gives you the ability to produce wealth, and so confirms his convent, which He swore to your forefathers as it is today. Deuteronomy 8:17-18 NIV** God has given us everything we are blessed to have and therefore when we tithe, we show our respect and love for the one who has blessed us. Tithing should come from your heart, out of love for God and not for what you will get back. It becomes important to recognize what has already been given to you. It is what you can give that will assist the poor, and those who don't know the Goodness of God, therefore to furthering God's Kingdom.

Remember this; Whoever sows sparingly will also reap sparingly, and whoever sows generously will also reap generously. Each man should give what he has decided in his heart to give, not reluctantly or under compulsion, for God loves a cheerful giver. And God is able to make grace abound to you, so that in all things at all times having all that you need, you will abound in every work. As it is written, "He has scattered abroad his gifts to the poor, his righteousness endures forever." 2 Corinthians 9:6-9 NIV

We must recall that grace is a gift from God and when we give back from our heart God is pleased. So maybe you can't start out giving 10%, try to give back something even if it's only 1%. I read from someone who said just get in the game. What is the game? It is giving back what has been so lovingly given to you. As you are able to give more from your heart, give it. Who knows, you may even surpass 10%. There isn't a percent on giving back to your Creator or to support others as long as it comes from the heart.

Remember, getting in the game is the most important element. So, get off the just sit on the sideline, and enter the game of giving, whatever the amount.

QUESTIONS:

1.   Why do you think you should tithe?

2.   Have you prayed to God about tithing?

3.   If you tithe, how has it changed your life?

4.   Do you see the difference from tithing and not tithing?

Lesson 2

Give Back to God

I know some of you are thinking, hey I gave my tithes what more do you want? Well, God doesn't just want your money, He wants you.   He wants the other gifts He has given you to be shared with others. Yes, giving your tithes is very important, but so is giving back your time to God. Well, first let's examine some of the things God has given you. He has given you life, health, family, job or career, education, and even more than has been mentioned as well as the ability to sustain them. When you think about all the time and blessings God has given to you even when you may not have deserved what He has given; that should move you to want to give back any way possible.

As a Christian Young Adult, you have the responsibility to acknowledge that all you have is not by your might, but because of the Lord. **The earth is the Lord's, and everything in it, the world, and all who live in it; Psalm 24:1 NIV** You don't have to be a millionaire to give back. There are other ways to give, there are your acts of kindness, time and just talking with someone can change a life. We find in the word: **In everything I did, I showed you that with this kind of hard work we must help the weak, remembering the words the Lord Jesus himself said: "It is more blessed to give than to receive." Acts 20:35 NIV**   We should commit to give God something, and time is just another way to show your faithfulness. God gives us choices. He doesn't make demands on us, but we should make the choice to show God how much we appreciate all He has given us. When we give to others we reciprocate the goodness God has shown to us. Each act of kindness, love, and sharing we give to others not only glorifies God, but also brings joy to others and ourselves. Let's not forget that: **You shall follow what is altogether just, that you may live and inherit the land which the Lord your God is giving you. NKJV 16:20**

QUESTIONS:

1. Why is it so hard to give back to God?

2. What have you given back or done for God lately?

3. How can you be a blessing to someone else by giving back?

4. How do you feel when you give back to God?

5. How do you feel when you show acts of kindness to others?

Lesson 3
Budgeting Your Life

We should spend no more than we make on a monthly basis. Ideally, that means to live on a cash basis and not use credit or borrowed money to provide normal living expenses. It also means that self-discipline to control spending and keep needs, wants and desires in their proper relationship.

Larry Burkett

We all get a rude awakening when becoming an adult means having adult responsibilities. Some of you may even start to experience these responsibilities in High School. You may start to help with the car payments or have to pay payments yourself. Then when you graduate from High School or turn of legal age some of you will have your own place or have to pay half the rent. There are the additional growing bills when you become an adult, or have adult responsibilities. You finally remember that money really doesn't grow on trees, like your parents or others have stated repeatedly, when you were a child. You wonder how you will be able to handle all these things and still tithe. As we discussed previously, you may have to start out less than 10% with your tithes and increase as you're blessed. You must actually sit down and look over your finances. Begin to write all of your responsibilities down. Yes, I did say responsibilities and not all those wants. After you have figured out the expenses which include your tithes, look at them and then seek God's guidance in handling your obligations. Once you put God first in guiding and directing your life, you show God your real priorities. When you trust the Lord with your finances God will help you to budget your money and help sustain you in every area even when there is mismanagement in your budgeting. For real, He will.

He can and will even and bless you with some of your wants. **And He said to them, "Take heed and beware of covetousness, for one's life does not consist in the abundance of the things he possesses." Luke 12:15 NKJV**

It's not just about the financial budget part of your life, but more so managing life. Before you take on your finances, you should put the effort into putting things in your personal life in order. After you decide to take charge of your life and set priorities then you can achieve great things personally and financially.

QUESTIONS:

1. Have you made a budget for yourself?

2. Do your expenses include more wants or needs?

3. Have you committed your budget to the Lord?

4. Are there ways in which you could improve on your budget?

5. What are some of the wants you would like to include in your budget after your needs are taken care of?

LIFE'S LITTLE CRISIS:

Let no man say when he is tempted, I am tempted of God; for God cannot be tempted with evil, neither tempteth he any man. James 1:13 KJV

We will always come across tempting situations, but we must realize God is not the author of that book. We are tempted because Satan knows that we are children of God and He wants to prevent us from receiving what is rightfully ours. Temptations come in all forms and there are some that will always continue generation to generation. You may already know what some of them are and we plan to look at a few. Some temptations experienced may be sex before marriage, drugs, peer pressure, violence, and drinking just to name a few. We must remember that in order to completely prevent temptation we would have to stay away, abstain and avoid at all cost. We need to prevent ourselves from being caught in these predicaments by being prayerful, staying in the word, and surrounding ourselves among other true Christians. However, in some cases, you can find yourself in these predicaments and you wonder how to fight these temptations of life that we may find ourselves. We need to step back and examine and ask ourselves these questions: Would God want us here? Would God be here? Would God be doing this? How will I like myself afterwards? If we answer no to any of the above then you know that it is not for you and God has something special planned for your life.

Sometimes we may find ourselves involved in abusive relationships. We are seeing more and more individuals involved in relationships that are abusive. We must realize that God didn't make us as a punching bag for someone else. God also did not intend for His children to be emotionally or mentally abused either. We are worth too much to God; we are the children of the King.

You must realize that if someone is abusing you it's never your fault though they try and make you believe such nonsense. Remember nothing you could ever do should give anyone else the right to be abusive to you in any form or fashion. If you are the abuser, or know someone who abuses, you need to seek counseling from God and a counselor. **The way of a fool is right in his own eyes: but he that hearkeneth unto counsel is wise. Proverbs 12:15 KJV**

Lesson 1
I am about to explode!

How many of you are experiencing or remember the peer pressure of High School or maybe even earlier in your life. There was and still is so much pressure on having good grades, looking good, being a great athlete, driving the nicest car, living in the nicest area, who you are dating, or if you were dating, getting the sweetest job, attending the best college, to do drugs or drink, to have sex or not, and so many others. You can't wait to get out of High School and be grown. Then when it finally happens you will come to find that the pressure continues and even maybe worse. You will still have pressure, but now it will be pressure of becoming an adult. The pressure of getting a job, finishing college or trade school, getting your own place, paying bills and even when will you settle down, etc. We have been asked these questions and more from friends, family, teachers, co-workers, and even strangers.

We adults have the pressure to succeed, achieve, and provide. We live in a world filled with the pressure of war, sickness, and death. You may have known people that gave into the pressure. I remember thinking about how my then 24 year old nephew had two friends that gave into the pressure and committed suicide. Here is my nephew just really starting out in his life and he already knew of someone that had committed suicide. These young people's lives had just begun when tragedy happened. They hadn't come close to reality of Adulthood when they took their own lives. They left loved ones, friends, future wives and future children behind all because they exploded from the pressure. We will never know what could have become of them as they matured. We will never know what a difference their lives would have made to us, or to the future. Now it has gotten even worse because suicide is affecting a much younger age group as young as 8yrs. of age. The scary part is a lot of it is due to bullying and with technology. Cyber bullying has made it relentless for kids to get away from being tormented.

Unfortunately, to these children and youth words can hurt to the very core of their being; to the point that they feel the only cure is suicide.

Some of you may have experienced pressure and unkindness by others. Some of you talked about it to someone, and others never said a word. Then there are those who have yet to experience any of these types' of experiences, but if in the future you do; remember it is important to find someone you can trust to talk with about what is going on in your life. Most importantly you must learn to talk with God and develop a true relationship with Him knowing that: **God has said, Never will I leave you; never will he forsake you. So we say with confidence, "The Lord is my helper; I will not be afraid. What can man do to me? Hebrews 13:5-6 NIV** Do not let other's words, or actions define who you are and what you can become; only God's words truly matter.

When you start to feel the pressure of life and feel like you are about to explode read this: **In my distress I called to the Lord; I cried to my God for help. From his temple he heard my voice; my cry came before him, into his ears. Psalm 18:6 NIV** Remember God never goes anywhere. He is there when you can't reach your parents, relatives, pastor, or even your friends. Just reach out to the Lord and He will help you defuse the explosion in your life. Before you explode and take away all that God has for you, and take away all you can give to the world, you need to stop and reach out to the Lord. Just call Him up and He will answer. **But they that wait on upon the LORD shall renew their strength; they shall mount up with wings as eagles; they shall run, and not be weary; and they shall walk, and not faint. Isaiah 40:31 KJV**

We have to realize that life will always have its challenges and how we confront them is what matters. You can allow them to defeat you, or you are can defeat the challenges. My choice is to believe that as long as the devil bothers me I must be doing something right; it's when he stops that I better worry. We have to be aware that when you are trying to become all that Christ wants for you, the devil gets angry.

The devil wants to steal our joy, peace, love, and understanding. He wants to take away all that God has for us and sometimes we let him win. When we allow circumstances to make us explode, we are giving the devil what he wants and he scores.

So when the pressures and emotions of life start to tear you down, think of these words: **Peace, I leave with you; my peace I give you. I do not give to you as the world gives. Do not let your hearts be troubled and do not be afraid. John 14:27 NIV**

QUESTIONS:

1. What pressure or concerns are you facing?

2. Do you know anyone who has been depressed?

3. Have you ever been so depressed that you have thought of suicide? If so what stopped you?

4. If someone who you knew was thinking of committing suicide, as a Christian what could you say to him or her if they reached out to you?

Lesson 2
Why wait? .... No one else is

You know how when you see that new game system, purse, that tight outfit or car; how you wanted to move into your own place to name a few maybe you know you can't afford to do any of the above right now. You decide that you will save your money until you can afford to make the purchase and the time is right. Then comes the time your purchase may require you to have put money down, or making a payment, sign an agreement, or maybe you need a co-signer. You don't mind taking on the responsibility because you will cherish and take care of it because this something special you wanted and earned. You saved and waited until it was the right time. Because you did, it meant so much more to you. Now if you had rushed in just because everyone else had a new car, a game, an outfit, or a new place before you're ready, you may not have saved enough or wouldn't have been ready for the responsibilities that come along with your decision.

You may be wondering why I used such an example to discuss voluntary sex before marriage. When you really want something special you need to wait, save, and abstain until the time is right. First and foremost having sex is more than just the act, for a lot of people it is very emotional. When someone gives of themselves in such a personal manner, they give themselves to another and it can't be taken back. **Flee from sexual immorality. All other sins a man commits are outside his body, but he who sins sexually sins against his own body. Do you not know that your body is the temple of the Holy Spirit, who is in you, whom you have received God? You are not your own; you were bought at a price. Therefore honor God with your body. 1 Corinthians 6:18-20 NIV** We must remember that sexual feelings can become confused with what we think is love. These are only temporary feelings and true love is a commitment that last for an eternity. Like we just learned our bodies don't belong to us; they are a temple of God and we must not destroy the temple He has given us.

I know you are thinking, but you just don't understand I love him or her and they say if we love each other we should take our relationship to the next level. I don't want to lose him or her to someone else who will give them what they need. There is nothing wrong with being in love, but when someone truly loves you they will respect your wishes to wait and understand your reasons for wanting to wait until you're married.

Real talk! I know what it is to be in love and I even know what is like to give your virginity away, before marriage. Yes, it may have felt good at that moment but it takes something away and every time that piece is given away, you can't get it back. Moreover, you can start over and refrain from sex until marriage. No, it can't return you back to virgin, but it can start the purity over again. See giving your body to someone doesn't prove your love, or will it seal the deal for them to never leave you. It doesn't fill the void you are missing in your life, or take away what happened to your life. Sex, like drugs is a quick fix for the moment and not a solution to what is bothering you. Sex can make you feel like everything is good, but when the moment is over the situations you are dealing with returns. Now it may be worse because you voluntarily gave away something special. I once heard someone say that when you have sex, you take on a part of that person and the more partners you have the more of others become a part of you. With that many people with you, how could you possibly have room for the right one? You will always be comparing each of your partners with whom you were with previously. By waiting there is no comparison, it's just who you love and who God brought in your life to be that special mate for your soul.

This is a difference from being physically forced to give your virginity away and giving freely. The sexually act wasn't your choice or your fault and you are not responsible for abuse. Now how you deal with the abuse afterwards to take away the shame and pain is your responsibility. Having more sex doesn't make it better or is cure. You can't put a Band-Aid on this type of a wound.

To clean the wound get the help you need to rebuild your life and don't complicate it more with sex. You can recover and have a wonderful life and soul mate with the help of professionals and the love and support of God and loved ones.

If you are thinking of indulging in sex by choice you need to take the time to get to know the other parts of your life first before you make such a strong commitment. When you do this step first it won't be sex, but making love to your spouse who really loves and respects you in every way and they will respect your decision and wait until you are married. God has ordained sexual activity belonging to those who are married in His sight. It's like having that special gift that you have saved to give to the right person only at the right time which should be on your wedding night. That doesn't mean getting married just to have sex. The love that is shared between a man and a woman who are truly committed to having a future together and ready for marriage is very special. You have a precious gift from God to offer on your wedding night that shouldn't be taken lightly. So, before you think about saying yes for the first time, or saying yes to someone again think about who gave you this precious body. You feel me?

It's never too late to start over and treat your body as a temple of God because you are a special gift that God has for that special someone at a special time your Wedding Day. When that day comes you will have a special feeling that you have never felt before in any previous relationships you will realize it was worth the wait. So let's take the step to wait. It doesn't matter even if you have already lost your virginity; you can start over by choosing to wait from this day forth for that special day. When you take, the challenge to wait it won't be easy. However, it will be well worth the reward. When the difficulties a rise take the time to reflect on past relationships involving sex and what the outcomes were and then decide, is it really worth a repeat performance?

Once you exhale you will find that the drama wasn't worth the few minutes or hours of pleasure and ended up still leaving you alone. If you wait to have sex you can become more complete because you are focusing on yourself and what you really need and want. When you become more mature to handle these emotions you will truly know what it means to give yourself completely to another. When the time is right with God, He will bless you with a wonderful spouse and Wedding night. It is worth the wait and so are you.

You and your chosen one have a responsibility to help one another to make the right choices. When someone loves you there is never pressure to change your decision, or belief on your body being a special gift and waiting. Oh I am not saying it will be easy and that feelings won't arise, but if that person is special to you, they will wait. Hopefully these verses will help you both.

Daughters of Jerusalem, I charge you by the gazelles and by the does of the field: Do not arouse or awaken love until it so desires. Song of Songs 3:5 NIV

How can a young man keep his way pure? By living according to your word. Psalm 119:9 NIV

God,
Let every teen and young adult realize his or her value. Help them to respect each other and the Godly life they are trying to live. Let them realize that in your word: "Everything is permissible for me"-but not everything is beneficial. "Everything is permissible for me"- But I will not be mastered by anything. "Food for the stomach and the stomach for food"-but God will destroy them both. The body is not meant for sexual immorality, but for the Lord and the Lord for the body.
1 Corinthians 6:12-13 NIV

Amen

QUESTIONS:

1. Why is it so hard saying no to having sex?

2. Now that you know you are a precious gift, can you wait?

3. Is it harder for men or women to wait? Why?

4. If you have already had premarital sex, do you think you could wait now?

5. What made you have premarital sex?

6. Did you regret having premarital sex? Why or Why not?

7. Did you feel pressured to have premarital sex? Why

Lesson 3
Stop the pain....Please

No! You don't deserve to be hit, slapped, and verbally abused, burned, shot, or misused. I don't care what you have said, done, or thought no one should misuse anyone that God created. God created the best and no one has the right to misuse His creation. If you love me you won't hit me; I learned that from the most loving being, my God. You see I want to be treated like my loving father has treated me.   He created me, nurtured me, loved me, forgave me, and blessed me. So, if someone who has done all of that for me and doesn't abuse me, then why would I let anyone else? One who is abusive could never love me as much as my God. To love me is to know that I am the Child of the King. If you can't treat me like a child of a King that I am then it is time for me to move on. I will not put myself in a relationship where there is no respect for who I am and who I come from. So, when you raise your hand and throw your insults you better look closely because you are seeing the God in me. Are you bad enough to hit God or bad enough to deal with the consequences from touching or hurting His child?   Each one of you came from God the King of Kings. Don't let anyone man or woman treat you with anything less than the best. Have the courage to get help and walk away. Remember; **For God has not given us the spirit of fear, but of power and of love and of sound mind. 2Timothy 1:7 NKJV**

The following ten facts are from Choose Respect's "Get the Facts: Dating Abuse Statistics" and "About Choose Respect: Dating Abuse Fact Sheet":

1. Each year approximately one in four adolescents reports verbal, physical, emotional or sexual abuse.

2. Approximately one in five adolescents reports being a victim of emotional abuse.

3. Approximately one in five high school girls has been physically or sexually abused by a dating partner.

4. Dating violence among their peers is reported by 54% of high school students.

5. One in three teens report knowing a friend or peer who has been physically hurt by his or her partner through violent actions which included hitting, punching, kicking, slapping, and/or choking.

6. Eighty percent of teens believe verbal abuse is a serious issue for their age group.

7. Nearly 80% of girls who have been victims of physical abuse in their dating relationships continue to date the abuser.

8. Nearly 20% of teen girls who have been in a relationship said that their boyfriend had threatened violence or self-harm in the event of a break-up.

9. Nearly 70% of young women who have been raped knew their rapist; the perpetrator was or had been a boyfriend, friend, or casual acquaintance.

10. The majority of teen dating abuse occurs in the home of one of the partners.

You have to realize that no matter how much you love someone you can't change someone unless they want to change. If someone is hurting you in any way, they need professional counseling. Until that person admits they have a problem and willing to seek counseling and start to turn their life around with God, they are no good for you now or maybe ever. That also includes anyone that you know that is abusive to another individual. They or you need to remove oneself from that situation. The best help you can be for someone is to pray for them and help them seek counseling. I know we always think if we love them enough that we can fix the situation, but sometimes love is not enough to turn things around.

We have to know that when someone abuses you there is a reason and love is not that reason. Bottom line…that person needs help. The best thing you can do is remove yourself from the situation, tell someone so that person can get the help they need. You cannot raise or change grown folk. Only God can change someone and that person has to let God in and allow Him to change their life.

If you are unable to remove yourself, immediately pray and make preparations. Make sure you know your surroundings, get out as soon as possible, and get help. Make sure that you don't return to that situation. Always remember you are never alone God will help you just call Him. You are special and don't let anyone take that from you by using you as a punching bag, and later saying I am sorry and I love you. Love doesn't physically abuse you. Real love doesn't hurt!!

God,

We pray for those who are facing an abusive situation. Let them know that they are precious in your sight. Give them strength and courage to walk away. Keep them safe and in your loving arms. Father give help to the abuser that they find you and get the needed help.

Amen

QUESTIONS:

1. Have you ever been in an abusive relationship or in one now?

2. If so, how did you get the courage to get out or to get the courage to leave?

3. Have you ever known anyone in an abusive relationship?

4. What would you say to someone who is in an abusive relationship?

5. Do you think there is something that may cause an individual to become involved in an abusive relationship?

6. How can we as Christians help each other feel better about ourselves?

Lesson 4

What are you high on?...

It is so easy to get caught up with the wrong things. We are living in a time of pressure. We all feel that if we just could get away from it and, or not think about all that is going on in our lives and in the world it will just go away. We are all in such a big rush and want everything right now. I have been guilty of putting so much pressure on myself to achieve certain goals in my life. When it took longer than I thought it stressed me out. It would have been easy to find a way to make it go away with drinking or drugs. But, when I looked around and realized the only drug I needed was to get high on God. When God becomes part of your life, He will put you on a high that no drug on this earth could ever give you. Then you don't have to worry about what you did or didn't do when you were high. You don't have to sell things or steal for this high. When you **Praise** the **Lord** in **Spirit** and in **Truth,** the feeling you receive is such a warm sensation. The feeling of God's Love embraces your entire being. When the Spirit fills your life you feel as if you can be and do anything. When you are around the Spirit that fills others, it is like experiencing a contact high. You can't help but feel the love and want to experience that same high. God's Spirit doesn't take away your thought process but increase your ability to do all things through Him. When you are high for God you are on the most wonderful ride you will ever take. God keeps you from the streets, not too the streets.

When the pressures of life weigh you down, and you feel as if there is no way out just try GOD. When you just want to escape and feel wonderful, children get your **PRAISE** on. I guarantee that you will experience no high better than being **high on God.**

Don't let anyone fool you drugs and alcohol can't take away your pain, problems, financial problems, loneliness, and abuse, it only covers it up and is only temporary. Nothing or nobody can do you like the Lord. God can take it away, forgive, and give you a new beginning. In the mist of your circumstances God can give you joy which can only come through your praise. I've tried Him-Why don't you?

So, what are you going to be high on and with whom? This should be a no brainer: **God** is the best **high** in the world. **For if ye live after the flesh, ye shall die; but if ye through the Spirit do mortify the deeds of the body, ye shall live. Romans 8:13 KJV**

QUESTIONS:

1. Have you ever tried drugs or alcohol? Why?

2. Do you know anyone who has a dependence on drugs or alcohol?

3. Why do you think there are so many Youth and Young Adults that feel they need drugs or alcohol to deal with situations?

4. Do you have someone you can talk with when you have a problem? Who?

5. When you go out, is a lot of alcohol or drugs being used? Why?

Lesson 5
I just want to belong

What is going on? There was a time when you only heard of gang violence in what people thought were bad neighborhoods. But now that it is hitting everyone people are saying there is a problem. As a teen-ager or young adult violence has been not only found in the streets or neighborhoods, but at home, at school, at play. Violence is hitting high schools, college campuses and even in elementary schools.   We are seeing gangs forming everywhere. You may be thinking we don't have them in our neighborhood or school but they are there, both male and female. First of all what is a gang? Webster Dictionary states: Gang-1. A group of people working or acting together; squad; shift. 2. A group or band 3. A group of people with compatible tastes or mutual interest who gather together for social reasons. 4. A group of youngsters or adolescents who associate closely, often exclusively, for social reasons, especially such a group engaging in delinquent behavior. The definition shows that a gang could be a good or bad group acting together to socialize positively or to attack negatively. Lately all we have seen are the bad groups which have taken lives in and out of schools. They have raped and attacked just because they feel in control.   We also have seen groups come together to show hate for different individuals and groups.

We ask ourselves why anyone would want to belong to such a violent group? The answer heard repeatedly is, I just want to belong. Isn't it sad that the only way someone can feel they belong or feel like they belong is by committing such awful acts? The thing that is most frightening is that you as teen or young adult could ever think that hurting someone just to belong is alright.

As teenagers and young adults wouldn't you rather belong to a group that is working together to attack the enemy; Satan. Jesus' Gang is the Alpha Omega which stands for the beginning and the end. God is our founder and leader. He is the beginning and the end of our lives. This gang loves, wants, and takes care of all its members. The blood of Jesus Christ who has died and rose again for our sins has already paid for your initiation. To join the Gang of Jesus Christ, all one has to do is: **Love the Lord your God with all your heart and with all your soul and with all your strength and with all your mind; and, "Love your neighbor as yourself." Luke 10:27 NIV**

In the Gang for Jesus you share love not hate and take care of others rather than hurting anyone. When we realize that every group out there isn't there to help you grow into all God has for you to become then you will seek the righteous one. Belong to something that uplifts you and not tear us down. You should become a part of something that you can be proud of that teaches values, morals, and love for one another no matter whom or where they come from. Now it is your choice to belong to something that doesn't take life, but brings life to Christ.

So, whenever someone approaches you just say hey, I already belong to a gang. It's the Jesus gang, and He is the beginning and the end. Ask God to help you explain to them that the gang you are part of loves life, and has no room for hate. Let them know that your initiation has already been paid through the blood of Jesus.

Let them know that their life has been spared to build a life; not take away life. God words let us know: **Be on your guard; stand firm in the faith; be men of courage, be strong. Do everything in love. 1 Corinthians 16:13-14 NIV**

God,

Help all the teens and young adults who feel like the only way to belong is to join a worldly group instead of seeking love, care, friendship through you. Give them the ability to refuse those attempting to take them from your arms. Please shower them with your love and protection each and every day

Amen

Questions:

1. Why do you feel it is so important to belong?

2. Do you know of anyone who belongs to a gang?

3. If you answered yes, do you know why they joined?

4. Has anyone ever approached you about joining a gang or group?

5. How did you respond?

Lesson 6
Violence is raging

This is what the Sovereign Lord says: You have gone far enough, 0 princes of Israel! Give up your violence and oppression and do what is just and right. Stop dispossessing my people, declares the Sovereign Lord.   Ezekiel 45:9 NIV

Every day be it newspaper, or media you find more violence being done to not only adults, but also now an increase of violence among teens and young adults. Not only are crimes being committed to teens and young adults, they are being committed by the same group. There is an increase of gang violence and sexual assaults. You can't even go to a party without wondering if you will return.

There is so little regard for human life. You hear gang members and some teens in general are saying they don't expect to reach the age of 21. It takes young people such as you to make a difference. You have to want more for yourself even if society is against you. It doesn't matter where you come from, the color of your skin, if you were brought up in a one or two parent home or raised by someone else. It's about saying that life is worth living and that you have more to give than take away.

You have the choice to become the answer to the question why has violence stopped raging. The reason that you are a part of the solution is because you are a child of God and your light has shinned so others can see that you don't have to be what the world thinks of you. You are what God thinks of you and that is good. Continue to shine to others in a positive way and let's stop the violence! Remember change can come from you. We all can make a change in the way society views us.

Questions:

1. How has the increased violence affected you?

2. How can we make a change that will decrease violence among youth?

3. Do you know of someone who has experienced violence?

4. Do you think society has contributed to the increase in crime? Why?

Relationships:

As Teens or Young Adults you will encounter many different types of relationships. How you handle the relationship as a Christian is different than the world may view handling relationships. In every relationship there is an opportunity to reach out in Christian love. In relationships we must realize that people come and go in our lives. Some people will disappoint us, but God's love will last forever. We must realize that we are only human; we make mistakes and so do others. We must put God first in all relationships where we chose to stay. God will bless your relationship if He is involved from its beginning and allow Him to bless the relationship. God has predestined certain people to enter your life, and then as human's we allow certain people to enter our lives as well as those forced in our lives or profession. It is important as Christian's to let God direct us through the relationships we encounter.

If you look back over previous relationships you have experienced; you should be able to look at which ones were of God and which of your own accord. We all have sat back and wondered how we ever let certain people ever enter our world. We must ask ourselves if we prayed over these entrances, or did we just open the door to allow anyone to enter? You must realize that the devil presents himself in many of forms including our relationships. He wants to destroy anything that is good. Ain't that nothing?

That is why you need to be very prayerful in your relationships. As yourself if this relationship is from God, or one you allowed entrance without God's guidance. As a Christian it is important to examine everyone you encounter with a Christian eye. I know it is difficult because you have no control at all times with whom you my encounter contact. There can always be unchristian individuals that may surround at home, at school, at play, at work, your Church, your family and even friends. That is why in everything you must pray, and ask God for guidance in any relationship. There is an old, old adage that says, "Trash gets in your eyes." This means that it is so important to know those with who you're involved. If you can consult God first; you won't be led astray.

Lesson 1
Friends Today, gone tomorrow

I can't even imagine where I would be today were it not for that handful of friends who have given me a heart full of Joy. Let's face it-Friends make life a lot of fun.

Charles Swindell

You will meet a lot of new people as you go through your life. Some will last forever and others will just be passing through.   But, the goal is to learn from each experience. We find that the friends we have, or had in High School may move on to other things or different relationships which may not include you. You may have even been the one to move on. Whichever circumstances you find yourself, always remember that the only true friend that last a lifetime is Christ.   He sees your faults and still stays.   He watches you make mistakes and doesn't judge you, but directs and helps you not to make them again. God forgives and continues to remain honest and true. He is not vengeful or a back biter.   For real though, sometimes the closest ones to you are the very ones that may hurt you the most. You don't have to worry about that with God. God will be your friend when you`re friendless, motherless, fatherless; when you have no sisters or brothers. You can share your dreams and tell your secrets to Him and you don't have to worry about them going anywhere. God is a blessing for anyone seeking a friend when they don't have one or you feel all alone, or even if you do have friends. God will still closer to you than anybody.

Some of us are blessed to have real true friends besides God and that is a true blessing. You should cherish that gift by being a true friend. If you seek God in your relationships and ask Him to bless you with special Christ like friends to be part of your life He will bless you in that area.

If you ask God to bless you with a true friend, you must pray that God will help you to become a true friend. **A man who has friends must himself be friendly, But there is a friend who sticks closer than a brother. Proverbs 18:24 NKJV**

QUESTIONS:

1. Do you have a close friend?

2. Have you ever prayed for a friend or friendship?

3. Have you ever been without friends? How did you feel?

4. How do you go about meeting or making friends?

5. Has anyone that you called your friend hurt you? How?

Lesson 2
Friendship made by God and, or through God

We all have had, or have friends, with certain qualities a friend should embody. When looking for a friend you should be looking for a Christian friend or a friend who exhibits **Christ like qualities.**

Loving	Proverbs 17:17; 1 Corinthians 13:4-7
Calm	Proverbs 15:1
Truthful	Proverbs 12:7; 14:5
Knowledge	Proverbs 10:14; 12:1; 13:16; 11:30
Trustworthy	Proverbs 11:13
Integrity	Proverbs 20:7; 11:3; 10:9
Peaceful	Proverbs15:1; 12:16; 22:24
Demonstrates Spiritual Fruit	Galatians 5:22-23

We must remember the friend we seek, or the ones we are blessed with should display these qualities and you also should be showing them as well. When demonstrating these qualities as a friend and they are demonstrated to you in return; your friendship is a true blessing. God's word **states: Do not forsake your friend and the friend of your father, and do not go to your brother's house when disaster strikes you-better a neighbor nearby than a brother far away. Proverbs 27:10 NIV** We have read in Proverbs the importance of a valuing friendship. We all can use a network of true friends for support and encouragement and we should give what has been received.

God,

We thank you for showing us the qualities of a true friend and how we can become a friend in Christian love. We pray that you will bless the friendships we have and those that are coming. We pray that they will always display Christ like qualities. Jesus name we pray….

Amen

QUESTIONS:

1. What kind of friend are you?

2. When you look back at these Christ like qualities have you found that in a friend yet?

3. Do your friendships have the above Christ like qualities? If yes which ones?

4. When you look at these characteristics do you see them in you and if so which ones?

Lesson 3
The-Hookup

There is a game called the hookup. It is about one individual looking to choose a date from three contestants of the opposite sex. Yes, I did say from the opposite sex. Remember opposites do attract. The procedure used in the hook-up is that the individual would ask several questions of each contestant. The one that answered the questions to the individual satisfaction was the one chosen to go on a date. Well, just like the game, as a Christian dating you need to ask several questions before you start dating an individual of the opposite sex. We must remember that dating is a preparation for those who wish to marry, or be in a serious relationship. You must seriously consider what type of dating is it serious, or platonic and make sure both parties are in agreement. However, you must become friends before you consider yourselves a couple.

As a Christian we should always think of God in choosing our dates you must be mature enough to ask the serious questions about their beliefs, family, friends, and about themselves. You should be strong enough to turn away from those that don't exhibit Christ like characteristics. We must be willing to commit our minds, body, conversation, and mate to Christ. We must realize that just because we are Christians doesn't mean that that we always act in a righteous way. It becomes hard at times to remain in Christ, when temptation crosses your path. That is why before you venture out on a date you need to take time to invite God along. God is the only one to help you stay focused on a Christian date. This doesn't mean you can't have an enjoyable date, but it does mean that your actions will reflect that of Christ. **Do not be unequally yoked together with unbelievers. For what fellowship has righteousness with lawlessness? And what communion has light with darkness? 2Corinthians 6:14 NKJV** Dates are steps to form the characteristic you want in a mate. When you go on dates you learn the traits you like, dislike and find out things that you enjoy doing. When you're dating it gives you a chance to see what you want in a mate.

Dating is the opportunity to meet new people of the opposite sex and getting to know the different personalities and to make new friends. When God is in the mix, one of those wonderful dates can turn into a love connection for life. But, you have to be willing to let God be a part of the dates you encounter and take each one as a learning experience. When you are mature enough and are prepared then the time will be right for marriage. The more time you spend with a God given he or she; each date you take is a step closer to a life time bond.

Dating for some may be a little hard. I can relate to that when you are a teenager be it male, or female dating can be a stressful time. For example, a female may be waiting to be asked out by someone special and for guys you are wondering how to ask someone out. Both of you are afraid of rejection which is very understandable. The most important thing is be friends first. When get to know someone as a friend first it makes dating so much more enjoyable. Get to know someone in a group setting. Learn if they are even someone you would want to take you out. You can learn a lot about someone when there is a group. You may find out that they're not the person you thought you saw. Once you get to know someone then it becomes easier for you to ask him, or her out or even turn them down if you decide that you want to just remain friends. You may even decide to step away from what you thought was the ultimate one.

Once you become friends first, you will always respect the friendship and value it at all times. See when you show respect and value then the treatment will be returned. We all want to be treated as God would. So, before you make that move or get so caught up in someone; take the time to become his or her friend first. Then if it's right to start dating you both will know. Let the dating begin and have a blessed time.

QUESTIONS:

1. Have you thought about what type of dating you would like to do?

Explain?

2. Have you ever invited God on your date?

3. Are you comfortable talking about God on your date?

4. As a Christian dating, what type of questions should you be asking?

5. What type of individuals do you date or you feel a connection?

6. How do you show respect for you and your date?

Lesson 4
Single and Mingling With God

I remember dealing with being single while in high school. It wasn't easy watched many people I knew were dating and I wasn't. I couldn't understand why that special person hadn't come along.   As I got older and entered college I dated more even got engaged.   Fortunately it didn't work out.   The older I became it seemed like more of my friends and family seemed to be married or getting; even those younger than me. I thought will that ever happen to me will marriage be in the cards. I decided to move out of state with my then 4yr old just to get a fresh start for my life. I know it may seem strange, but even after all the adult things I had been through I didn't grow up until that move. Once away I become more involved in knowing God and getting closer to Him. I really began to examine myself. I finally learned to be content with myself and improve in areas of my life that needed improvement. Then the realization hit until there was peace in myself I wasn't ready to be with someone in a committed relationship. I also learned to depend more on God to make me complete rather than having someone else to do that in my life. I learned that the reason I hadn't found someone special was because I wasn't ready or a complete person myself.

When God presents the perfect mate you should be a complete person for him too. You both should enhance each other and not try to complete one another. I wished those lessons were known to me earlier. Then maybe I could have avoided a lot of bad relationships. I tried to find something in them that would complete me which was already in me, but hadn't been developed. I wanted to find the love form them that I was lacking in myself. It's not just about finding someone special, it's about being someone special no matter if you decide to stay single, or you ask God to bless you with a date, or mate. God is always on time.

We all know that being single can be hard. You may start to question what is wrong, why I can't find that special someone, or will I ever. Some of you are saying I don't care about being in a serious relationship or getting married. I like being single. Whatever is your way of thinking the most important thing is that right now you are single. Even if you are thinking about getting married or you're engaged to be married, weigh all your options. Until you say I do before God you are single. Since you are single it's time to mingle with God. You can devote all of your time getting to know and pleasing just Him. When it's right, if it's right; you'll know…God will tell you.

God's word states: **I would like you to be free from concern. An unmarried man is concerned about the Lord's affairs-how he can please the Lord. But a married man is concerned about the affairs of this world-how he can please his wife - and his interest are divided. An unmarried woman or virgin is concerned about the Lord `s affairs: Her aim is to be devoted to the Lord in both body and spirit. But a married woman is concerned about the affairs of this world-how she can please her husband. I am saying this for your own good, not to restrict you, but that you may live in a right way in undivided devotion to the Lord. 1 Corinthians 7:32-35 NIV.**

When you are single you are able to concentrate on God. When you are involved in a relationship, or marriage your attention becomes divided. You need this time is getting to know God and yourself in your singleness and oneness. Think of being single as a time of reflection and improvement with help from God. Learn to love yourself as God loves you. Find out what makes up your being and discover what makes you happy and complete? Take the time to better yourself, so that best in you comes shining through for all to see.

Being single is a time to invite the Lord into your life and enjoy all that He has planned for your future. Having a single status doesn't mean you are unlikable, unlovable, or even unwanted. It means that someone much more important needs your full attention. At this very moment you need this time to develop into that special person that He created and allow Him to share all of His knowledge with you. In the midst of this time, you can also find out if you want to be involved in a relationship, marriage, or even staying single. Being single and mingling with God gives you prospective on all areas in your life. Most of all this time gives your undivided attention to God. When He has your attention then you can learn of Him and all that is in store for your destiny. So let's get ready to mingle all you singles.

My purpose is that they may be encouraged in heart and united in love, so that they may have the full riches of complete understanding, in order that they may be know the mystery of God, namely, Christ, in whom are hidden all the treasures of wisdom and knowledge. Colossians: 2:2-3 NIV

QUESTIONS:

1. What can you do to improve your relationship with God?

2. What personal things could you work on to make you complete?

3. Have you shared with God what you would like in a mate?

4. Is it harder being single and a Christian? If so why?

5. Are you ready to mingle with God while you are single?

6. Why do you think it is better to be single at this point in your life?

Lesson 5
Are you Relationship or Marriage Material?

One day you may say to yourself, you know, I want to get married settle down and start a family with the one I love, my soul mate. The question is: are you marriage material?   We all want to find Mr. or Mrs. Right, but are you Mr. or Mrs. Right for them? Most of you have certain qualities you are looking for in your soul mate. Let's just look at what some of those qualities may be:

Appearance:
He or She better have a look that is appealing to me. I am looking for someone who is well groomed, keeps himself, or herself in shape, dresses nice, etc. You know you see appearance before you get to know them.

Achievements:
He or She should be educated with a college degree or trade, with a good job, they have better be making bank. They need to be intelligent, sophisticated, have their own place and own transportation. They have to be on the same level as me and able to take care of a family and me.

Other Characteristics:
They need to be spiritual, no kids, or one child, never married or married only once, older than me, same age, or younger etc.

We have so many things we look at when choosing a mate. Let's flip the script. All these things that you are requesting from a mate do you possess them too. How can we really expect to find these things in someone else if they can't see them in you? The mate God has for you is to complement what you already have going for yourself.

The question should also become: What are you bringing to the table?   It is not always about money, but more importantly the traits that you bring to enhance the possible union. Do you convey a complete person relying on what God has blessed you with? Are you bringing the qualities of a friend? Are you carrying the love of God and family in you? Are you presenting the best of what God has in you to the table? Could you instead display confusion, dishonesty, need to take, but not to give, and unwillingness to work together? Asking for something you are not willing to give leaves you with nothing. **"Haven't you read," he replied, " that at the beginning the Creator made them male and female' and said, "For this reason a man will leave his father and mother and be united to his wife, and the two shall become one flesh? So they are no longer two, but one, Therefore what God has joined together, let man not separate."** **Matthew 19:** 4-6 **NIV**

Whether you have just started dating or looking for a long-term commitment both require you to bring the best of you to the table. We must realize that dating prepares us for going into a long-term relationship. As a teen or young adult, this is the time to get to know who you are and what characteristics you are looking for.   As you mature, the characteristics become more developed, because you have grown. You then move into a more committed relationship which is preparing you for the ultimate commitment for marriage. At this point, you should know about yourself and be ready to settle down with one person. When you reach this point in your life you should know what you want out of life and have started pursuing your goals, or have achieved some of them.

Now is the time to develop the characteristics that will make you someone to date, or marry. Just remember if you model yourself after your heavenly Father, you will be the hottest thing and ripe for the picking.

QUESTIONS:

1. Have you talked about your future husband or wife with God?

2. What are you looking for in a future husband or wife?

3. Have you found your soul mate? If so, how do you know?

4. What do you have to offer your future spouse?

5. Have you lost your future spouse because you were asking them to fulfill what was missing in your own life?

6. Is there something on your list of qualities you are looking for in your future spouse that you could change now? Why?

Lesson 6
Forgiven.... But not forgotten

We have discussed different types of relationships and seen that importance of some and the unimportance of others. No matter what relationship you encounter there may be problems, or situations which require forgiveness. How do you forgive someone who hurts you so deeply by words, hands, deceit, gossip, backbiting, actions, lack of love, and not being there for you, etc.? How do you forgive someone so close to you such as a family member, friend, spouse, child, co-worker, and even yourself? **Therefore, as God's chosen people, holy and dearly loved, clothe yourselves with compassion, kindness, humility, gentleness, and patience. Bear with each other and forgive whatever grievances you may have against one another. Forgive as the Lord forgave you. And over all these virtues put on love, which binds them together in perfect unity. Colossians 3:12-14 NIV** We as Christians have a charge to forgive as Christ has forgiven us. We all have made mistakes and it was and is by the grace of God we were forgiven. We must let go of trying to settle the score and let God fight our battles.

Okay, so you learn to forgive, but how do you forget? We are human and unlike God who said: **"I, even I, am he who blots out your transgressions, for my own sake, and remembers your sins no more. Isaiah 43:25 NIV** It is very hard to forget things that have happened. It may seem the more we try to forget the harder it is to do. We tend to recall the circumstances that lead up to the incidence in order to help us not find ourselves repeating again. We must realize that forgiving someone does take time, but prayerfully with God's help you will forgive, and maybe even forget. We should not let the recollection of what happened consume us. We must learn to remove the toxic from our spirit before it destroys who we are and whose we are. We are children of a most forgiving Father. Just like our earthly parents have forgiven us even forgotten; there are some situations that aren't forgotten but used as a lesson to reflect on not to condemn us but to make sure not repeated.

I don't want you to get the wrong impression. It is not always that easy to forgive someone, but slowly you need to start by doing so you are not letting it become the focal point of your life.

Life is too short to spend on situations or people that can take you away from the pleasure life has to offer you that follow Christ. Don't let anyone take away all that God has blessed you with or future blessings. Why don't you start today by forgiving others which includes yourself as well. **For if you forgive men when they sin against you, your heavenly Father will also forgive you. But if you don't forgive men their sins, your father will not forgive your sins Mathew 6:14-15 NIV**

You have a future of magnificent blessings; don't let the past keep you away from your future. Let go and let God handle those who have wronged you. I guarantee that His punishment will be far more devastating than anything you could think, do, or say. I read somewhere that Forgiveness is giving love where there is none. So, go out and give love to those who needed the most, the ones that set out to hurt you. Give love to the ones that don't recognize that they hurt you. Spread the love that God gave you when He forgave you of your sins. Don't think that gives anyone to hurt you, but forgiving puts you above the hurt and makes you stronger. Besides, life is too short for all that negativity.

If you are blessed to have the opportunity to forgive; then the love that was given to you when God forgave you is shining through. No it doesn't mean you are letting them get away with it; if you get a chance tell them how you feel and then let go. A lot of times it's not getting the chance to let someone know how his or her actions affected you. If you don't get the opportunity talk to God and then let it go. You will be happier for it. Remember forgiveness is for you not the other person. It is so that you can move on to greater and bigger things that God has in store for you. Once you have let go of the negative that is holding you back you will like yourself even more.

QUESTIONS:

1. Has someone ever done something you need to forgive him, or her for?

2. What was the relationship of the person or persons to you?

3. Is it harder to forgive someone close to you? Why?

4. How do you know if you've truly forgiven someone?

5. Has God ever forgiven you for something? Why?

Family Dynamics:

Each one of us has a story to tell about our family. Some have wonderful stories and times spent with their families. While others may feel as if they didn't really have a real family. It may be because it was not their biological family, or they weren't close. However if you really look back and realize that growing up may not have been quite the way you wished it could have been; guess what, you are still standing. If you look back you may even find some good memories. All families have problems no family is perfect.

Families come in so many forms. You have your biological, adopted, and even extended family. All families are made up of different individuals and personalities. We can't always choose our family dynamics, but we can make the choice of how to become part of the family.

Some of you that may have lived with an extended family consisting of: grandparents, aunts, and uncles instead of your biological parents. There are also others who may have been a special blessing for someone who couldn't have children of their own, or who had so much love that they wanted to share with you.

When we look at our families, it's just like belonging to the family of Christ. God is our Heavenly Father and we all are adopted into his family. We all have different gifts, personalities, abilities, needs, and experiences. Together we make one big wonderful family. We all have our faults and shortcomings, but by the grace of God, He allowed us to belong.

Your family may be traditional or unconventional and by working together it can be just as wonderful as being part of God's Family. We just have to learn to appreciate those who love us enough to give us a chance at having a family. You have to learn that being a part of a family takes working together, sharing, and loving one another. Most of all we need to show respect for one another. Remember no matter how God brought you together as a family you are one now and it's time to act like it.

Lesson 1
You just don't understand nor do
you?

How many times have you said the above statement to a parent, grandparent, or guardian? It feels as if they are living in a different time, than yours, or even a different planet. They don't understand the pressures you are going through, or do they? If you would ask them they would probably say they felt the same way about their parents, grandparents, or guardian.   As a youth you think that they don't understand your feeling just because they don't agree with you.

Parents are unique. As teens, or young adults in that both are coming from their side. Perhaps both sides need to take time and examine what the other is saying. As a parent, myself in my younger years, I always told myself that I would be different from my parents. Yes, in a lot of ways, I am, but in the values and training that was given to me we are the same. The things that I couldn't stand are the same things I require of my own children. God is our heavenly Father and there are things that He also requires of us that we may not like, but are what we need. I know that it is easy to believe that our parent's don't have a clue and it doesn't change the older we get. Believe it or not, they have been through a lot of the things we have and they have more than a clue of what you think they don't understand.   They may not know how to come to us with advice, but they really do understand a lot more than we give them credit for. **Train a child in the way he should go, and when he is old he will not turn from it. Proverbs 22:6 NIV**

You have to remember that parents are people too, and they did and still do make mistakes just like you. It's up to both of you to take the time to really communicate with each other. A lot of times they don't understand because you won't let them into your life.

It hurts them when you talk to everyone else about your feelings except him or her. You have caused them to now they walk in the darkness of your life.

As a parent I observe how teens and young adults speak and act towards their parent's. Things have changed a lot since when I was growing up. Today there is no respect shown to our elders and as far as respect that is out the window. I would have never been able to speak to my parents or elders the way your generation does. Then you wonder why parents treat you the way they do. I believe to get respect you must earn respect. To be treated as a young adult you need to act like one.

You must realize that your parents, elders and guardians have a lot of rich knowledge to bestow on you if you take the time to talk with them. When you really talk with them, that means attitudes dropped, you will find out that they have experienced a lot of the same things as you. Times may be different and more challenging for you now, but time just repeats itself. Only when you as a teen, or young adult allow your parent's entrance into your life will there be understanding.

When you are blessed to have parents that give you love and guidance you are blessed. They not only provide you with the necessities of life, but give you so many of your wants, don't you think they deserve the respect and admiration they are due? Teens and young adults in America feel that they deserve to have what they want, when they want at no cost to others. Unfortunately, society's mentality has been dropped in your laps. We have forgotten that everything you get, someone had to pay the price to obtain. Your parent's have worked hard to provide for you and when you show disrespect to them and shut them out it hurts the relationship.

You would be surprised of the number of teens and young adults out there wishing they had parents to care about their lives, wanting to know who they hang out with and where they're going. These same individuals like you, are longing to have someone to talk with and be there for them.

So, while you may think your parent's wouldn't understand your feelings or what you may be going through the reason may be because you won't include them in your life. Now maybe it's time for you to reflect on how you have treated your parent's. They may not be the coolest, but their love for you is never changing even when they don't like the direction or choices you are making. Let's bridge the gap and become a family that can love and respect each other and who knows things could change for the better. Isn't it worth a try to be all that God envisioned a family to be?

Children, obey your parents in the Lord, for this is right. "Honor your father and mother"- which is the first commandment with a promise-"that it may go well with you and that you may enjoy long life on the earth." Ephesians 6:1-3 NIV

Questions:

1. Do you have a good relationship with your parent's? If not, why?

2. Do you ever feel that your parents don't understand? If yes, why?

3. Do you feel you show respect to your parent's? If not, why?

4. Do you think your parents feel you understand them?

5. How can you make your relationship better?

Lesson 2
Why did you hurt and then leave me?

I understand that it may be hard to respect a parent that abandoned, abused, or mistreated you. But, you have to remember that they are the vessels used by God to bring you into the world and anything coming from Him is outstanding. So despite how or who you came from, just remember they were the vessel which brought a new beginning starting with you. Out of the ashes of despair comes new life which is yours. Now you have a chance to become what your parent's couldn't or have not been for you.

We spend so much time hating those we felt did us wrong that we can't live the life that has been given to us. Yes, I said hate. Webster's New World Dictionary says: hate- means to have strong dislike or ill will for: to wish to avoid. If we look at how much energy we use to hate someone; we could channel that energy to build you up. The time that you have wasted on hating someone who is not even worthy of your time hasn't hurt them, but hurts you. When you spend so much of your life hating the person that brought you pain, you are giving them even more power over your life. I am not saying that what they did was not wrong, but the best revenge is living a life full of richness and full of God. When God is part of your life you will let Him fight your battles and you will allow the hate to turn into love. You may never want to be around that person, but you will love them enough to pray for their very soul that hurt you. When you let go of the hate, it doesn't give them your approval for what has happened, but it gives you the ability to move forward.

Once you can move forward then you break the bonds of the hurt and pain. You may never forget completely, but it will not consume your life and cripple your growth. You will take all those negatives and turn them into positives. You will have grown stronger from your past and be able to show others that may be going through the same that you can come out of it a winner too.

Don't let the disappointment, pain, and anger keep you from not understanding that there is a purpose for your arrival. So, let all these negative feelings go and know these words from God are true as is His love for you. **And the God of all grace, who called you to his eternal glory in Christ, after you have suffered a little while, will himself restore you and make you strong, firm and steadfast. 1 Peter 5:10 NIV**

QUESTIONS:

1. Have or do you know anyone that has been abandoned or abused?

2. If so, by whom was the abuse?

3. Who helped you or someone you know handle what happened?

4. Have you been able to get passed what happened?

5. How did you survive?

6. How has what affected your life changed you?

Lesson 3
You're not really my Parent....

He predestined us to be adopted as his sons through Jesus Christ, in accordance with his pleasure and will. Ephesians 1:5 NIV

For me as a parent it was a wonderful and special time when I adopted my son.   I always wanted him to know that he is just as wonderful to me as giving birth to my daughter. His arrival was not the same, but the outcome was. I have been blessed to be a parent to two great blessings from God. You may be thinking, sure you are just saying that when you know one child came from you and the other came to you. This is true, but I love them both and each one has a special story to tell of their arrival to our family. It's not how you arrived, but why you are here. The reason is because of the abundance of love that we wanted to share by having children in our lives. God blessed me to become a parent.

The best story ever is when God blessed Mary with Jesus; Joseph wasn't his biological father, but he loved Jesus as one of his own. We are all are adopted into the family of God through His son Jesus. That is something special that can never be compared with how we arrived, but the way to our arrival. So, in the eyes of God we are all adopted. Go figure....

You should never think you were unloved because you are adopted. It takes love for someone to allow another person to take you as his or her child. This type of love is unconditional when you want more for your child, then you could give, or feel that the environment is not for a child. It takes unconditional love to bring any child into your life and home. Think of adoption as just another avenue to bring a child into a family as Christ was the vessel to bring us into the family of God.

Questions:

1. Are you a child that is adopted?

2. How do you feel about being adopted?

3. Do you ever wonder why you were put up for adoption?

4. Have you thought about searching for you biological parents? Why"

5. Do you feel different than other children or siblings you may have?

6. Do you feel love from your adoptive parents?

Sharing the Word

We all have a responsibility as a Christian to spread the good news about Christ, and all He has done for you all of us. You know when you hear a good song you've heard or an excellent movie you have seen how you spread the word? As Christians we need to spread the good news so others can see or listen to what God has to say. Well, you should have that same excitement when you share the news of the love of Jesus Christ and all He has done for you. We must realize that we are all evangelists for the Lord. As the seasoned saints use to say, we may be the only Bible someone will read. When you share your blessing and who blessed you, this is a way of expressing the word of the Lord with others.

However, before you can truly share the word you must accept the Lord as your own personal Savior. Once you have accepted Christ you should join yourself to other children of God's kingdom. Being with other Christians gives you a group that can encourage and help you along your journey in Christ. I once read this statement: It is in the midst of the people of God that He refines and develops your Character and sends you on your mission to spread the word. Spreading the word doesn't mean forcing the word on someone; God doesn't force His word or will on us. God invites us to learn more of Him, by how He treats and loves us. The same way that God has blessed you can be shown in how you express His blessings by the telling of His goodness. This spreads God's word faster to those who don't know Him for themselves. Are you ready to accept the mission or will you allow the blessings God has for you to self-destruct? **It was he who gave some to be apostles, some to be prophets, some to be evangelist, and some to be pastors and teachers, to prepare God's people for works of service, so that the body of Christ may be built up. Ephesians 4:11-12 NIV**

Lesson 1

Love one Another

"By this all men will know that you are my disciples, if you love one another." John 13:35 NIV

It is sometimes easier to love strangers than it is to love your brother. People have the misconception that a Christian will be so lovable. As humans with different personalities and moods it can be challenging. There is a difference in saying you're being a Christian and being Christ like. When you accept Christ into your life and become a part of Church, or Christian group you expect others to be Christ like in every way. Yes, it is very upsetting when you realize that they are not acting Christ like and it also very disappointing when you see more of the world in their actions and personality then in the unbeliever. The one thing I have learned through encounters is that we can't allow those who make the choice to let the devil enter into them ruin your relationships with those who really do exhibit Christ like attitude and actions. Trust me when I say it is very challenging to move past their human worldly characteristics to love them, but we must realize that once you become a Christian you still have to work at taking on Christ like behavior. When you run across someone like that you truly must stay in prayer for him or her. We must still learn to love our fellow brother. You may not like their ways, but we must love them anyway.

God does not like all of our ways, yet He sent His only son to take away our sins because He loves us and He wanted to take away those bad qualities. As followers of Christ we must let our love over shadow our feelings and reach out to all mankind in brotherly love. It may be difficult to accomplish that hurdle with attitudes, personalities, and ungodly actions. We still need to reach out to others, and show and sharing **Christian Love** just as God reached out to us. Situations and circumstances will come across your path those that will not allow you to show or share **Christian Love** that is when you let go and let God and just pray for them. The most important thing is to give **Christian Love** regardless of the outcome here on earth. Your blessings come from God and not man.

QUESTIONS:

1. Do your actions show Christian love to your fellow brother?

2. How do you go about spreading the good news?

3. Is it hard to love someone who doesn't show love towards you? Why?

4. Has someone who confesses to be a Christian showed you a different image? How did that make you feel?

5. How can we move past feeling and still show love?

Lesson 2
So, you want to join?

I remember when I was in college; I wanted to join a sorority. I wanted to be a Delta, and that was all I could think about. I wanted to achieve the goals that those so together women seemed to have achieved. I was willing to do whatever was required of me to pledge the sorority. In time I achieved the goal of sorority hood. It wasn't easy and it required much dedication, time and energy. I had to learn the history of the sorority; I had to show love for my sisters and it was hard to love someone who was demanding so much from me. Plus it was a group of women and we know with that comes different personalities, interests, abilities, and their own opinions. I had to also remember they had the power because they were my big sisters and my line sisters. When it was all said and done we all had one thing in common, we wanted to be Delta's and once the pledge period was over, we become one body. As a Delta, I have a sisterhood of great women no matter where I go, young and old. We have a love for what we have accomplished, who we are, and for each other.

I use this example for you to see that becoming a member of God's Church takes the same dedication that joining any sorority, or fraternity and you receive even greater rewards. When you make a choice to become part of such an exclusive group you must take the time to learn the history through reading hearing and studying God's word. We must go through the pledge period before we are able to go out and witness to others though our testing and knowledge we are acquiring about God. When that final day of commitment comes we become part of the most precious sorority, or fraternity; The Eternal Kingdom of God. In this kingdom we all have different personalities, abilities, interest, and opinions, but our main objective is to have God say, **"His master replied, "Well done, good and faithful servant! You have been faithful with a few things: I will put you in charge of many things. Come and share your master's happiness!" Matthew 25:21 NIV**

There is nothing wrong with becoming a member of an organization that shows togetherness and Christian love, that God would approve of; just remember there is nothing more important than wanting to be members of God's Kingdom. Once you are a member then you're always a member. No matter how long it's been since you attended a meeting, even if you forget some of the history; you can always go back because you are a member for life and no one can take that away from you. Accepting God and striving to do His will is the greatest pledge one cold ever make. Stomp for God!!

It's time to reach out and invite others to become long time members of God's Family. He is the **Alpha** and the **Omega,** the beginning and the end. So let's get stepping.

Questions:

1. What are you willing to give up in become a member of God's House?

2. How can you invite new members to get to know Christ?

3. Can you spread the news in your surroundings? How?

4. If not, why?

5. Are you a proud member of the Alpha Omega chapter in God's House? If not why?

6. What types of organizations do you belong to? Why did you join?

7. Is God part of the group, or groups that you are involved in?

Lesson 3
Praise God I belong; what's next?

> **Christ had made all things right.**
> **I had nothing to do but accept it as a**
> **gift from Him.**
> **Hannah Whitall Smith**

Now that you are a member you must continue to read and study your history of God just as you would for a fraternity, or sorority. You should join a church and get involved in the many activities that can bring you closer to God and give you fellowship with others who truly worship God. Remember, the more you give, the more you receive. The more involved you become the closer you find yourself to Christ. When you say you belong to a group there should be some evidence of your membership. I know we get busy with our everyday lives, but we must remember who provides us with this life. Whether you are going through something or coming out of troubled time your family should be there to help you in your time of need. We should look out for one another and not being envious, or unkind. God put us here to join with each other to make a great Kingdom for Him. The only way we can do this is to learn to love one another as He loves us. As a fraternity, or sorority when you mention you belong, there is a sense of love with each other, because it is known what you have been through to become a member and what it takes to stay one. We have so much pride to say we belong to a Greek organization or any group we should take even greater pride to say we belong to Christ and we are His children.

When you look back over your life God has blessed in so many ways. A true testament to His goodness is through our works. You belong to a precious group of people and as a member it is your obligation to spread the news, get involved in those areas that can help you achieve that goal and work harder to know God.

Give to those who don't know God and continue to work at giving back to those who do and still need support from a member of God's group. Every time you look at the color red think of Christ who shed His blood for us. God loved us enough to send the most precious gift, His darling son Jesus to wash away our sins. The act was more than an obligation; it was the ultimate sacrifice. Wow that's real love!!

Now, you know the answer to the question what's next? You better get busy, times a wasting. There are new members to find and stories to share. Each day is a time to share your love of God with others. You don't have to preach to people in order to bring them to Christ. The life you live, the love you give, shows everyone that God abides in you. Just continue to learn and give your all at becoming more like Christ and let the world see who you are by your actions and words. Remember, eyes are watching those professing to be a Christian child of God. What do you want them to see?

But now God has set the members, each one of them, in the body just as He pleased. 1Corinthians 12:18 NKJV

QUESTIONS:

1. So, what are you going to do now that you are a member of the exclusive group of Christ?

2. Where do want to spend your eternity?

3. Are you a member of a church?

4. Are you active in any groups at church? Which ones?

5. If you answered no above then why not?

Conclusion

As we conclude our study, I pray that God's Love will surround, engulf, and move you. I know that we may not have covered all the areas that you may encounter, but remember that in all you may go through God is the answer. The more you learn about Him the more you grow and the stronger you become. Let all that we have discussed and you have experienced guide you through your incredible Teen or Young Adult Life. Remember who you are and whose you are. Commit to memory that your Heavenly Father is almighty and everlasting.

Don't forget these words: **If my people, which are called by my name, shall humble themselves, and pray, and seek my face, and turn from there wicked ways; then will I hear from heaven, and will forgive their sin, and will heal their land. 2 Chronicles 7:14 NIV**

God,
We ask that your words will become a light to our path and lamp to our feet on this journey. We pray that you will engulf us with your love, so we will know how truly special we are. We ask that you will guide our footsteps and let us realize what a wonderful Creator you are. Assist us in sharing your word with others. Help us learn that all we have means nothing if we don't have a true relationship with you. Let those who don't know you realize that an eternal life with you is priceless. In Jesus name we pray.

Amen

Resources:

Join **S.U.G.S.** (Secure, Unique, Gifted, and Spiritual Centered) Young Ladies. For more information: **www.expressionsoflife.org**

What is an Eating Disorder?
Some Basic Facts

Eating disorders such as anorexia, bulimia, and binge eating disorder: include extreme emotions, attitudes, and behaviors surrounding weight and food issues. Eating disorders are serious emotional and physical problems that can have life-treating consequences for females and males.

ANOREXIA NERVOSA is characterized by self-starvation and excessive weight loss.

<u>**Symptoms include:**</u>

Refusal to maintain body weight at or above a minimally normal weight for height, body type, age and activity level
Intense fear of weight gain or being "fat"
Feeling "fat" or overweight despite dramatic weight loss
Loss of menstrual periods
Extreme concern with body weight and shape

BULIMIA NERVOSA is characterized by a secretive cycle of binge eating followed by purging. Bulimia includes eating larger amounts of food-more than most people would eat in one meal-in short periods of time, then getting rid of the food and calories through vomiting, laxative abuse, or over exercising.

Symptoms include:

Repeated episodes of binging and purging
Feeling out of control during a binge and eating beyond the point of comfortable fullness
Purging after a binge, (typically by self-induced vomiting, abuse of laxatives, diet pills and/ or diuretics, excessive exercise, or fasting)
Frequent dieting
Extreme concern with body weight and shape

BINGE EATING DISORDER (also known as **COMULSIVE OVEREATING**) is primarily by periods of uncontrolled, impulsive, or continuous eating beyond the point of feeling comfortably full. While there is no purging, there may be sporadic fast or repetitive diets and often feeling of shame or self-hatred after a binge. People who overeat compulsively may struggle with anxiety, depression, and loneliness, which can contribute to their unhealthy episodes of binge eating. Body weight may vary from the norm to mild, moderate, or severe obesity.

OTHER EATING DISORDERS can include some combination of the signs and symptoms of anorexia, bulimia, and/or binge eating disorder. While these behaviors may not be clinically considered a full syndrome eating disorder, they can still by physically dangerous and emotionally draining. All eating disorders require professional help.

SYMPTOMS OF DEPRESSION

●Adolescents

Drop in grades or conduct
Low self-esteem
Fatigue
Changes in sleep patterns
Self-destructive behavior
Inattention to appearance

Source: "Help Me, I'm Sad," by David Fassler, M.D. and Lynne Dumas

GENERAL SIGNS OF ALCHOLOL OR DRUG USE:

Schoolwork has declined; grades suddenly slipping or dropping
dramatically   Missing school (skipping secretly or "sick" to go)
Mood changes (irritable, crying jags) Dropping out of usual activities
(music, sports, hobbies)
Physical appearance changing; (poor hygiene, unusual style changes)
Friends suddenly change; doesn't introduce, new friends
Money or valuables missing from parent's purse, from home
Furtive or secretive behavior (e.g., bedroom door locked and takes long
time to answer)
Hostile, aggressive outbursts
Seems to have "lost" motivation
Forgetfulness
Unusual sleeping habits (changing over time or dramatic)
Depressed
Anxious
Something just doesn't seem right

Internet sites:

Alcoholics Anonymous
www.aa.org

National Eating Disorders Association
www.nationaleatingdisorders.org

Rape, Abuse, Incest National Network (RAINN)
www.rainn.org

Suicide Awareness
www.save.org

Numbers:

National Center for Missing and Exploited Children
1-800-843-5678

National Domestic Violence Hotline
1-800-799-SAFE (7233) TDD 1800-787-3224

National Eating Disorders Association
1-800-931-2237

National Runaway Hotline
1-800-RUNAWAY (1-800-786-2929)

National Suicide Prevention Lifeline
1-800-273-TALK (8255)

National Youth Crisis
1-800-442-HOPE (4673)

RAINN (Rape, Abuse, Incest, National, Network)
1-800-656-HOPE

This section is for those of you who have never had the opportunity to write, or draw in a journal. For those who don't know about journaling; it is a constructive way to express one's self. When you write or draw, it gives you a vessel to express your emotions, dreams, disappointments, and most of all celebrate your accomplishments. When you communicate through journaling, or drawing; it releases all the inner thoughts that had no outlet. When you begin to create you go to a special place where there is no right, or wrong way to express yourself in a quiet atmosphere.

I have enclosed a few starters to help your release your feelings either by writing or drawing. I want you to read the starters and take a few minutes to allow yourself to feel what the words are speaking to your soul. Then take a few pages to write down what emotions the words create in you.

After you have had a chance to express yourself the remaining pages are provided to give you the vessel needed to channel your emotions, thoughts, and dreams. I hope that this will be the beginning of the rest of your life. My prayer is that you have experienced a renewing of your mind, spirit, and soul.

When the storms of life are raging

And wars and violence are waging.

Boys and girls losing their innocence

While others are just losing common sense,

I trust in God to stand by my side

As I take this Christian ride.

So Dear God I pray that you help me to stay

Far away from trouble that comes my way.

For all these blessings I truly pray.

Wanda Maria Phillips

The Life Decisions Journal

When I take the time to express myself I find the way too
 help myself.
 Then I can become what God sees in me and all that I was created to be.

Wanda Phillips

When I look in the mirror what reflection do I see looking back at me? Is it my past pain, or just my shame?...................

Oh my dear, it seems to appear that it's time to choose a career.
Are you just lost, or just too scared to be the boss……..?

All I want you to do is say I love you.
Every day I wait just to hear you say I love you.

Have you heard that it now time to spread the word......?

How much does your worth measure?
Isn't it precious treasure?

You are now entering your own personal space. This is where you can be free to express yourself by writing, or drawing your thoughts and feelings.

Now it's time for you to take this journey to explore your inner most thoughts, dreams, accomplishments, hurts, joy and sadness, etc. I want you to discover all that God has for you and your life. Take the time to look back and reflect on your growth, then move forward and leave the past mistakes and pain in the past. Remember your past doesn't determine your future, or destiny. You can choose to stay in the past or decide to venture into your potential. You should think on the positive not the negative. It will not always be easy, but the more you step forward the greater the reward.

God,

We pray that the journey we are moving towards brings the glory not only to you, but also to our lives. Help us to share our feelings in this journal as a way to begin the healing and start our journey to a full and wonderful life. In the name of Jesus we pray.

Amen

Journal Entry

Journal Entry

Journal Entry

Journal Entry

Journal Entry

Journal Entry

Journal Entry

Journal Entry

Journal Entry

Journal Entry

Journal Entry

Journal Entry

Journal Entry

Journal Entry

Journal Entry

.

Journal Entry

-

Journal Entry

Journal Entry

Journal Entry

Journal Entry

Journal Entry

Journal Entry

Journal Entry

Journal Entry

Journal Entry

Journal Entry

Journal Entry

Journal Entry

www.ingramcontent.com/pod-product-compliance
Lightning Source LLC
LaVergne TN
LVHW061224060426
835509LV00012B/1410